UWEM ESSIA

FIREARMS, GENDER VIOLENCE, AND THE PURSUIT OF EQUALITY

Mainstreaming Gender in Conflict Prevention and Small Arms and Light Weapons (SALW) Control Book 3

Dedicated to a Peaceful World Where the Rights of all Gender Groups are Equitably Considered and Respected

Contents

Preface

In today's world, where violence and gender inequality continue to cast long shadows over societies, the intersection of firearms, gender violence, and the quest for gender equality remain an urgent matter of concern. The book "Firearms, Gender Violence, and the Pursuit of Equality," explores the critical confluence of themes, dissecting its complexities and exploring the pathways toward a more equitable and secure world.

Across eight chapters, the book embarks on a journey that starts with the realization that gender-based violence remains an insurmountable barrier to achieving true gender equality. Chapter One presents statistics to support the view that more women worldwide have experienced physical and sexual violence than men, and firearms all too often play a role in these tragedies. The chapter explains the link between firearm ownership, domestic violence, and the quest for gender equality, emphasizing the grave implications of firearms misuse.

In Chapter Two, the focus shifts to small arms control in the context of organized crime, unraveling how illicit SALW poses threats to international security. The chapter further emphasizes the importance of comprehensive measures and international cooperation, shedding light on how the United Nations Convention against Transnational Organized Crime and its Firearms Protocol offers a glimmer of hope in a world grappling with this challenge.

Chapter Three introduces the MOSAIC compendium as a toolkit designed to combat the misuse of and trade in SALW. It details the collaborative efforts of twenty-four partner entities within the UN system and outlines the interconnectedness of gender equality and reducing illicit arms flows, as envisioned in the Sustainable Development Goals.

The subsequent chapters take us on a journey through conflict zones

(Chapter Four), governance strategies for small arms and light weapons
(Chapter Five), post-conflict regions (Chapter Six), and the aftermath of
the Kosovo conflict (Chapter Seven), all through a gender-focused lens.
These chapters underscore the crucial roles of governments, civil society,
regional organizations, and international entities in promoting gender equality, women's rights, and a more secure future for all.

Chapter Eight explores the South African experience with small arms
regulation and its impact on gender violence, revealing insights into how
policy development and implementation can affect firearm-related deaths
and ownership. This chapter, like others, spotlights the multifaceted interplay
between societal norms, legislative frameworks, and the pivotal role of gender
perspectives in shaping outcomes.

This book seeks to inform and inspire, offering a wealth of knowledge,
perspectives, and empirical evidence to prompt informed discussions and
action. It reminds us that the road to gender equality and the elimination of
gender violence is laden with complex challenges and intricate details. However, it also presents the way forward, illuminated by the collective wisdom,
cooperation, and dedication of individuals and organizations committed to a
brighter future.

As we embark on this intellectual journey, we ponder the interplay between
firearms, gender violence, and the pursuit of equality and explore the myriad
opportunities that exist for effecting change. May the insights and ideas
shared in this book catalyze a world where pursuing gender equality is not
just a distant aspiration but a living reality for all.

INTRODUCTION

In a world grappling with the pervasive shadow of gender-based violence and persistent disparities between genders, the subject of firearms looms as a contentious and compelling issue at the heart of the pursuit of gender equality. "Firearms, Gender Violence, and the Pursuit of Equality" embarks on a critical exploration of the intricate connections between these themes and the various intersections that shape our shared human experience. Today, we find ourselves at a crossroads where global efforts to achieve gender equality coexist with deeply rooted issues of gender-based violence. These issues encompass a broad spectrum, from physical violence to sexual abuse, leaving indelible scars on the lives of countless women worldwide. Notably, firearms serve as catalysts for escalating conflicts, endangering the lives of women and girls in their own homes.

Chapter One explains how women worldwide have encountered physical and sexual violence, with firearms frequently entangled in such incidents. Firearms misuse emerges as a prominent factor in the realm of gender-based and domestic violence, presenting a grim paradox to a world striving for gender equality. This chapter not only exposes the harsh truth but also lays the foundation for our exploration of the multifaceted dimensions of this issue, highlighting the alarming prevalence of firearms in domestic violence-related homicides and the global challenge of a "gun culture." However, gender perspectives remain underrepresented in national and international documents, showcasing a pressing need for in-depth exploration and understanding.

Chapter Two explains the intersection of small arms control and the challenge of containing organized crime. Illicit SALW is a formidable threat to international security, driving the need for comprehensive countermeasures, strong national legislation, and advancements in criminal justice systems. We delve into the vital role that international cooperation and information-sharing play in addressing the access of criminal groups to these weapons and scrutinize the United Nations Convention against Transnational Organized Crime and its Firearms Protocol as critical players in this complex equation. The significance of integrating small arms control, women's rights, peace, and sustainable development is underscored, demonstrating the increasing recognition of their interdependence. In this intricate web of interconnectedness, the chapter also introduces the essential concept of gender-responsive small-arms programming and the profound influence of gender analysis.

Chapter Three unveils the Modular Small-Arms-Control Implementation Compendium (MOSAIC), a voluntary toolkit designed to combat the illicit trade and misuse of small arms and light weapons. Over a decade of coordinated efforts within the UN system, engaging 24 partner entities with diverse expertise led to the development of this valuable resource. MOSAIC aligns with key global agreements and contributes to the Sustainable Development Goals, particularly Goal 16. Through this lens, we understand the integral connection between gender equality and reducing the illicit flow of arms. Chapter three explains gender mainstreaming as a pivotal strategy for ensuring that small-arms control initiatives consider the consequences for individuals of all genders. In the broader context, this chapter compels us to examine the intricate interplay between masculinity, small arms, and violence, a crucial facet of long-term strategies for violence reduction.

Chapter Four invites us to explore various weapons collection programs, unveiling voluntary initiatives such as buy-backs, amnesty periods, exchange programs, and collective development endeavors. These programs are tailored to reduce the presence of small arms and light weapons in conflict zones. However, the effectiveness and challenges associated with their implementation are crucial areas of exploration. Chapter Five shifts our focus to the central role of governments and civil society organizations in SALW control. Governments are tasked with promoting gender equality, involving women and men in decision-making, establishing coordinating bodies, and addressing gender aspects in their strategies. Civil society organizations dedicated to gender issues have emerged as a force for promoting local ownership and influencing policies in small-arms control, disarmament, and peace-building programs.

Chapter Five discusses what small arms control stakeholders need to do to check SALW proliferation and gender-based violence. First is the cross-border nature of small arms and light weapons issues. Second is the role of the United Nations and the imperative of integrating gender considerations into SALW control projects and programs, emphasizing the need for gender-specific data collection, support for civil society organizations, gender training, and coordinated efforts through the UN Coordinating Action on Small Arms (CASA) mechanism. Third is the role of donors and UN agencies in promoting gender equality in arms control interventions. Donors are urged to encourage governments to fulfill international agreements related to gender issues, provide capacity-building support, and ensure that gender perspectives underpin their initiatives. The United Nations Development Program's (UNDP) Eight-Point Agenda for Gender Equality in Crisis Prevention outlines various aspects that encapsulate the broad reach of gender considerations.

Chapter Six explains promoting gender sensitivity in post-conflict regions. An empowerment approach focuses on the central role of women's empowerment in the more significant development context. Non-governmental organizations emerge as an indispensable force in addressing gender-based violence in these post-conflict regions, filling gaps left by government efforts. Reproductive health and society have become pivotal points of discussion, shedding light on the challenges faced in post-conflict regions due to war-related difficulties and deeply entrenched social norms. These regions often contend with inadequate reproductive health education, limited access to contraceptives, and other intricacies that demand attention. The case of Bosnia and Herzegovina gives insights into the persistent problem of family violence, where various studies reveal the extent of domestic violence. SOS telephone services and non-governmental organizations are crucial pillars of support for victims.

Chapter Seven unfurls the complex history of Kosovo, marked by cultural, religious, economic, and political tensions that intensified during the Kosovo Conflict in the 1990s. Women who bore the brunt of the conflict's impact experienced displacement, hardships, and unique challenges within a profoundly patriarchal society. Efforts to address reproductive health for women, economic disparities, and the multifaceted challenges faced in the job market and family structure are explored in Chapter Seven. Minority women in Kosovo face unique challenges, struggling with underrepresentation in leadership positions and relying on support from the international community to overcome these obstacles.

Chapter Eight reviews South Africa's experience with the Firearms Control Act (FCA) enacted in 2000. The FCA bestowed law enforcement agencies with the power to remove firearms from individuals embroiled in domestic violence, underscoring the Act's potential to impact individual lives positively. This chapter delves into the persisting high rates of gender-based violence in South Africa, from female homicide rates to widespread gender-based violence, highlighting the role of firearms misuse in these harrowing incidents. This chapter also unearths the influences of global, regional, and national developments on South Africa's firearms legislation, revealing the significance of the UN Firearms Protocol and the Southern African Development Community's (SADC) Firearms Protocol. Successful gun control movements in Canada, the UK, and Australia are also spotlighted as influential factors that have shaped South Africa's policies. It also explains how, initially, the FCA led to a decline in gun homicides, particularly in cases of intimate femicides. However, a subsequent breakdown in enforcement and governance led to increased firearm availability, contributing to a recent surge in firearm-related violence.

This book provides a comprehensive look into the intricate relationships between firearms, gender violence, and the pursuit of gender equality, fostering an environment for informed discussions and action. It offers critical reflections on SALW proliferation and checking gender-based violence, challenging existing paradigms and laying bare the interconnectedness of these critical issues with peacebuilding.

CHAPTER ONE: FIREARM OWNERSHIP, DOMESTIC VIOLENCE, AND GENDER EQUALITY

Summary of Chapter One

1. Gender-based violence is a significant barrier to achieving gender equality, with nearly 30% of women worldwide experiencing physical and sexual violence, often involving firearms.
2. Firearms misuse is a significant factor in gender-based and domestic violence, significantly increasing the risk of violence escalation in households where perpetrators have access to firearms.
3. About one-third of domestic violence-related murders involve firearms, with women being the primary victims.
4. The "gun culture" in some countries, including Serbia, is a significant obstacle perpetuated by societal memories and a climate of insecurity.
5. International frameworks acknowledge the gender aspect of firearms control, but gender perspectives are underrepresented in national and international documents.
6. Serbia has established legal frameworks and regulations for firearm ownership, but enforcement and gender considerations are areas that require improvement.

Gender-Based Violence and Firearms

Gender-based violence against women remains one of the most pervasive barriers to achieving gender equality worldwide, endangering the lives of women, children, families, and the safety of entire communities. Globally, nearly 30 percent of women have experienced physical and sexual violence at least once in their lives, with intimate partner violence being the most common form. Women are the primary victims of gender-based and domestic violence, and available data indicate that firearms misuse is a major causal factor, adversely impacting the lives of women and men differently, particularly in the context of domestic violence and intimate partner violence. In households and relationships where perpetrators have access to firearms, the risk of weapon misuse and violence escalation increases by up to five times. The consequences of such misuse are severe due to the lethal potential of firearms, resulting in a higher likelihood of fatal outcomes or injuries with long-lasting consequences, such as disability. High fatalities occur with GBV and DV in private settings where victims lack the means to escape attacks.

Available evidence indicates that about one-third of all domestic violence-related murders involve firearms, and the majority of victims are women. Most incidents involving men and women killed with firearms occur within their homes or yards. Fatal outcomes resulting from firearms misuse are more frequent in domestic violence cases than in other forms of criminal violence. Firearms are not solely used for homicides; they are also employed for intimidation, threats, psychological abuse, sexual violence, and exerting control over victims. Addressing the complex issue of domestic violence and gender-based violence necessitates a comprehensive approach that harmonizes various laws, regulations, strategic documents, and policies across different jurisdictions. It is thus necessary to incorporate gender, gender-based violence, and domestic violence aspects into the broader strategy of weapons control while also considering how weapons relate to gender equality and violence against women.

In many countries, the extant laws recognize the connection between firearms misuse and domestic violence, which, to some extent, has contributed to reducing the number of homicides involving firearms to some extent. However, the situation remains challenging, especially in the countries facing post-conflict conditions. Challenges persist, preventing complete and adequate protection. The reported cases of domestic violence are increasing each year, yet they represent only a fraction of the problem's accurate scale. The presence of firearms in households or their accessibility to perpetrators instills fear in victims, discouraging them from seeking help from authorities and deterring potential witnesses from reporting the crimes.

When crimes are reported, over half of them are rejected due to insufficient evidence or victims' unwillingness to testify. This rejection does not imply that the violence did not occur but instead did not result in institutional intervention. This situation hampers the effective enforcement of existing laws and institutional procedures aimed at punishing perpetrators and providing long-term protection for all individuals exposed to violence.

A joint research effort of UNDP and its national partners in Serbia seeking to reduce the risk of firearms misuse in the context of domestic violence, particularly gender-based violence, and aiming to improve legislative and strategic frameworks, enhance prevention measures, and raise awareness among men, women, girls, and boys regarding the risks associated with firearm misuse found an undeniable correlation between firearms and GBV. The project aligns with Goal 4 and aims to reduce the risk of firearm misuse and strengthen victim protection systems, thereby increasing trust among victims and citizens to report gender-based violence and domestic violence. The project builds on solid evidence of the correlation between firearm possession and domestic violence, data on the misuse of weapons in domestic violence, information about the substantial number of firearms owned by civilians, and crime rates in the Western Balkans compared to neighboring countries. This research involved analyzing the national legal framework's compliance with international agreements binding on Serbia and European Union (EU) law, which Serbian law had to harmonize with during negotiations. The analysis aimed to identify areas for improvement, ensuring that national legislation addressing firearms issues is both gender-sensitive and sensitive to the correlation between gender-based violence and firearms. The results are summarized below:

The Connection Between Firearms and GBV

The undeniable correlation between firearms and GBV reveals a grim reality.

- Women constitute about 64.2 percent of all victims killed by a family member, while men account for 35.8 percent.
- Intimate partners are responsible for 42.2 percent of murders committed within families, with women falling victim to their partners in a shocking 88.1 percent of cases, compared to 11.9 percent for men.
- In situations involving family members, 31.2 percent of these homicides involve firearms, and women represent 63.2 percent of victims killed by a family member with a firearm, in stark contrast to 36.8 percent for men.
- An overwhelming 91.1 percent of individuals killed by a partner wielding a firearm are women, with men comprising only 8.9 percent of such victims. In cases of intimate partner violence, 39.4 percent of women are killed with a firearm, and a staggering 51.9 percent of GBV incidents involving firearms result in death. The likelihood of death due to firearms misuse in GBV cases is three times higher than in criminal contexts.

Combating Domestic Violence and GBV

The persistence of a "gun culture" is a significant obstacle rooted not only in traditional values but also in citizens' mistrust of institutions. This culture remains resilient due to societal memories, particularly during periods of low personal security, high crime rates, corruption, and a climate of impunity for violence. Media reports on firearms misuse in DV and GBV often fall short, presenting firearms merely as tools of violence without delving into the underlying issues. Firearms are typically portrayed within the context of "traditional values."

In Serbia, existing data and statistics, particularly those related to criminal offenses, are insufficiently informative and lack categories relevant to firearms misuse. For instance, data from the Statistical Office of the Republic of Serbia and the Ministry of Justice do not contain information about firearms-related measures and risk assessments despite their importance. Furthermore, laws do not mandate recording data based on risk factors. Data collection methods related to GBV and DV are complex, with femicide being considered not only the most severe form of domestic violence but also a homicide offense. Similar complexities exist for other forms of DV, such as injury infliction and sexual violence. Data from the Ministry of Interior in 2016 reveal that women were victims of firearm-related homicides in 21.2 percent of cases and suffered firearm-related injuries in 16.6 percent of cases.

Strategic approaches to firearms control have thus far insufficiently leveraged the gender dimension, women's participation, and diverse perspectives and needs of women, men, girls, and boys. The gender mainstreaming of policies must extend beyond data classification and firearms analysis. It should encompass women's involvement in the firearms control process and decision-making related to firearms control, GBV, and DV. Gender mainstreaming in firearms control necessitates dismantling the entrenched "gun culture" and associated gender roles in Serbia.

The Legal Framework Governing Firearms Possession and Use

The legal framework governing firearm purchase, possession, and carrying, reasons for firearm confiscation, conditions for carrying service weapons, and firearm storage methods, among others, require a thorough analysis and potential improvement to prevent violence committed with firearms, DV, and GBV. Additionally, laws related to institutional responses to DV and GBV and penal policies need redefinition, especially given the current leniency in DV cases.

A strategic approach to the intersection between SALW and GBV necessitates data that are currently unavailable. Achieving a strategic approach relies on evidence, which, in turn, relies on facts and numbers. Therefore, it is imperative to enhance the monitoring and data collection systems related to weapons and violence committed with them, as well as establish a coherent system for recording and monitoring GBV. This system should facilitate collaboration among various entities dedicated to combating GBV.

Firearm Ownership, DV, and GBV – Lessons from Serbia

In 2016, Serbia was home to approximately 618,061 registered firearms in civilian hands, with 23,539 owned by private legal entities (non-state entities). Estimates of service weapons suggest about 900,000 firearms. In 2016 alone, over 10,000 weapons were seized, with a mere 744 of them being illegally held, indicating that the majority of arms used in Serbia are from official sources. A substantial segment of Serbia's population legally possesses, carries, and uses firearms. Authorization extends beyond military and police personnel, encompassing members of various security agencies, customs officers, individuals involved in detective work, court guards, private security companies, forest guards, gamekeepers, and those managing hunting grounds. A sizeable number of individuals without specific professional requirements maintain firearms in their households, authorized by competent authorities. This widespread civilian ownership stems largely from self-defense concerns, reflecting a degree of public distrust in institutions.

It is evident that the 'gun culture' persists in Serbia, symbolizing masculinity and protection in society. This cultural element is deeply rooted and has historical and patriarchal underpinnings. Men overwhelmingly dominate firearm ownership, accounting for 94.7 percent of firearm owners, as well as the majority of both perpetrators and victims in firearm-related crimes. Remarkably, 78.8 percent of homicide victims involving firearms are men, while 83.4 percent of firearm-related injuries affect them. Conversely, women constitute a mere 5.3 percent of firearm owners, and they disproportionately experience firearm-related crimes, with 21.2 percent of female victims of firearm-related homicide and 16.6 percent suffering firearm-related injuries. Efforts to address this cultural pattern are crucial. Firearms control forms an integral part of Serbia's strategic objectives, aligning with EU regulations and international treaties on arms trade and gender-based violence (GBV).

Generally, gender perspectives in firearms control are underrepresented in national and international documents. They are primarily limited to recognizing women as victims of firearm-related crimes, encompassing domestic violence, war crimes, and crimes against humanity. The consideration of men's and women's distinct needs concerning weapon control is only marginally addressed, while gender balance in decision-making processes regarding firearm control remains notably absent.

Recognition of Gender Concerns in International Firearms Control Frameworks

International frameworks, such as the UN Program of Action on Small Arms and Light Weapons (PoA), acknowledge the gender aspect by expressing concerns about the impact of illicit arms trade on women. However, these documents lack specific information about gender aspects. For example:

- The Arms Trade Treaty mandates the consideration of GBV and violence against women and children in export assessments. The Security Council Resolution 1325 emphasizes gender integration in traditionally male-dominated fields, including armed conflicts and peace-building processes. It underscores women's participation in decision-making processes and their protection against violence.
- The Committee on the Elimination of Discrimination against Women (CEDAW) recommends focusing on preventing conflicts and violence, regulating arms trade, and controlling the circulation of conventional weapons. The proliferation of conventional weapons, tiny arms, can directly or indirectly affect women as victims of GBV and domestic violence.

- Sustainable Development Goals (SDGs) prioritize gender equality and gender aspects in arms control and reducing the number of weapons. Target 5.2 aims to eliminate violence against women and girls while ensuring their participation in decision-making processes. Target 16.4 focuses on responsive, inclusive, and representative decision-making.
- The EU Strategy against Illicit Firearms, Small Arms, and Light Weapons and Their Ammunition, introduced in 2018, includes the principle of incorporating a gender perspective into firearms control. However, this principle needs to be developed in the strategy.

Serbia's national documents predominantly adopt a protective approach, emphasizing the correlation between firearms and women's security and protection against violence. They provide minimal attention to a participatory approach. In practice, the lack of comprehensive data and records on the relationship between GBV and firearms in Serbia hinders the effectiveness of even the protective approach. Despite efforts to address the gender dimension in firearms control, there is still work to be done to ensure a more gender-sensitive approach. Encouragingly, Serbia's National Action Plan for the implementation of Resolution 1325 aims to introduce a gender perspective into all public policies related to defense and security. It also seeks to improve the safety and security of women employed or engaged in the security sector, as well as investigate and prevent violence against women effectively. The Serbia NAP acknowledges the need for research on women's security, improved regulatory frameworks, and increased women's participation in peace and security processes. One noteworthy activity in the Plan involves taking measures to confiscate firearms or restrict access to firearms for perpetrators of violence.

Data from Serbia, as reported by SEESAC, reveal that firearms are frequently involved in incidents related to domestic violence. In 2019, 18 incidents of domestic violence involved firearms, with male perpetrators (97 percent) far outnumbering female perpetrators (3 percent). A total of 210 victims were identified, with the majority being male (80 percent) and 43 (20 percent) females. These incidents resulted in deaths, suicides, and injuries, with firearms often used as a threat. The probability of death due to the misuse of firearms in domestic violence cases is three times more common than incidents in a criminal context. Serbia ranked 17th out of 48 countries in terms of female homicides involving firearms between 2007 and 2012. From 2012 to 2016, there were 84 homicides committed with firearms, with 21 percent of victims being women. During the same period, 35 women and 186 men were injured by firearms.

Acquiring, owning, and carrying firearms with authorization from competent authorities

The Arms Trade Treaty, ratified by the Republic of Serbia in 2014, sets general rules governing arms acquisition and trade. It aims to establish high international standards for regulating the international trade in conventional arms, preventing illicit arms trade, and curbing the diversion of arms to unauthorized users. While the treaty provides a framework for states to regulate arms-related issues such as the acquisition, possession, storage, marking, and destruction of arms, it also allows significant discretion for states to enact specific regulations. This approach is based on principles like the right of all states to individual and collective self-defense, non-interference in the internal affairs of states, and respect for states' legitimate interests in acquiring conventional arms for self-defense and peacekeeping operations. States are required to implement the treaty consistently, objectively, and without discrimination. They must also establish and maintain national control systems and control lists to implement the treaty's provisions.

Similarly, European Union (EU) law establishes minimum standards for various aspects of arms control, which are binding on EU member states. As Serbia is in the process of joining the EU, it is obligated to align its legal system, including regulations related to arms control, with the EU acquis, which comprises legally binding EU documents governing arms control. The EU Directive 91/477/EEZ, as amended by Directives 2008/51/EEZ and 2017/853/EEZ, sets standards for the acquisition and possession of firearms classified as category B. It permits individuals aged 18 and above (except for hunting and target shooting) to acquire and possess such firearms if they have legitimate reasons and do not threaten themselves, others, or public order. The directive also allows minors to possess firearms with parental consent or supervision from an authorized adult. It emphasizes the importance of monitoring and periodic reviews of firearm permits. It requires states to establish rules for controlling firearms and ammunition, as well as safe storage measures to prevent unauthorized access. Specific authorization for owning and carrying arms is summarized below:

- The Action Plan for Chapter 24 - Justice, Freedom, Security, highlights the need for a more efficient system of controlling firearms acquisition, storage, transfer, and trade to reduce the misuse of illegally possessed firearms and enhance public security. However, this action plan does not address gender-related aspects or adequately focus on conditions for firearm ownership and carrying, particularly regarding the correlation between GBV and firearms.
- The Roadmap for a sustainable solution to the illegal possession, misuse, and trafficking of SALW and their ammunition in the Western Balkans by 2024 plays a crucial role in improving arms control in Serbia. It aligns with the UN Program of Action on small arms and practical disarmament measures and aims to harmonize arms control legislation with EU regulations and other international obligations. This Roadmap includes goals related to raising awareness, educating the public about firearm dangers, advocating for arms control, and integrating gender and age concerns into small arms and light weapons/firearms control policies.
- The Strategy on Small Arms and Light Weapons Control in the Republic of Serbia, built upon the Roadmap, recognizes the gender perspective in understanding the possession, use, misuse, and effects of small arms and light weapons. It emphasizes measures to prevent violence against women, domestic violence, and other forms of GBV. Activities include aligning the legal framework with international and European regulations on firearm acquisition, possession, and carrying, adopting bylaws, and

enhancing public awareness about the link between GBV and firearm possession. The strategy's effectiveness will be assessed using key performance indicators, some of which incorporate gender-sensitive aspects.

Serbia's Law on Weapons and Ammunition

The primary law governing firearm acquisition, possession, and carrying in Serbia is the Law on Weapons and Ammunition. This law classifies firearms into four categories (A, B, C, and D). Category B firearms can be acquired, owned, and carried with authorization from competent authorities. Individuals seeking permits for category B firearms must meet several conditions, including demonstrating a justifiable reason for firearm possession, passing medical and psychological assessments, and having no violent criminal history. Minors may possess but not purchase firearms under parental supervision or at licensed training centers. Collector's permits, allowing individuals to own multiple category B firearms, are available for those meeting specific criteria.

Firearms may not be carried in public places unless individuals hold valid permits. Permits for carrying firearms are issued to those with a genuine need for personal security. Such permits are granted for a limited period and have specific restrictions to ensure public safety. Carrying permit holders must conceal their weapons publicly and not cause public disturbance. The law obligates firearm owners to handle their weapons carefully, store them securely to prevent unauthorized access, and ensure they do not endanger public safety or property. Competent authorities are responsible for regularly verifying compliance with these conditions and revoking licenses if necessary. While the law prescribes penalties for various firearm-related violations, such as failing to renew medical certificates or violating storage and handling requirements, the practical enforcement of these regulations needs to be more consistent, and there needs to be more enforcement related to medical practitioners' obligations.

Overall, Serbia has established legal frameworks and regulations regarding firearm acquisition, possession, and carrying, with provisions that address public safety and potential risks. However, the effective enforcement of these regulations, particularly regarding medical and psychological assessments, remains an ongoing challenge.

The Law on Weapons and Ammunition, supplemented by relevant bylaws, regulates two critical conditions: physical fitness and the manner of firearm storage.

Physical Fitness for Firearm Possession and Carrying: The Rulebook on determining the physical fitness of an individual for possessing and carrying firearms stipulates that individuals are deemed physically fit to own and carry firearms if medical examinations confirm their physical and mental health, with no medical conditions that would make them unfit for firearm possession. If an individual is found "unfit," the authorized health institution must inform the person examined and the nearest Ministry of Interior unit. An unfit individual cannot undergo a new evaluation for six months. Any change in the health condition of a licensed firearm owner must be reported promptly by the practitioner. The medical certificate of fitness includes an examination report by a selected practitioner, not older than 30 days, anamnestic data, clinical examination by a health team, including a psychiatric or neuropsychiatry assessment, psychological interviews, and personality assessments.

Manner of Keeping Firearms Secure: The Regulation on Premises and Technical Arrangement for Secure Storage and Keeping of Firearms and Ammunition mandates that individuals purchasing firearms or applying for collector's permits must ensure safe storage conditions, making firearms and ammunition inaccessible to unauthorized persons. These items must be locked and isolated in secure cabinets, safes, or similar containers within residential or other authorized premises. However, this regulation lacks a detailed definition of how firearms should be stored in residential buildings.

Legal Requirements for Firearms Ownership and Possession

The Law on Weapons and Ammunition mandates individuals who previously held weapons carry licenses and permits to request the necessary documents, along with a medical fitness certificate, by a specified deadline. Persons with licenses for trophy weapons must re-register, sell, deactivate, or surrender their weapons within a year of the law's enactment. Those with licenses for hunting weapons with unlabeled barrels must submit the required documents within six months from the law's enforcement.

While significant improvements have been made in regulating firearms acquisition, possession, and carrying, some shortcomings persist in the Law on Weapons and Ammunition:

- The law does not include specific provisions to address emergencies related to domestic violence or protective measures against violence under family law as grounds for permit denial.
- The law lacks detailed provisions governing the behavior of firearm owners within their private spaces and does not establish protective measures or sanctions for owners disturbing family or household members.
- The law does not specify the roles and duties of specialists and other health workers in providing information about patients authorized to own or carry firearms or regarding changes in their health conditions.
- Security vetting procedures are outlined in the Law on Police but offer police officers discretion in selecting information sources. There is no obligation to consult family members or investigate dysfunctional family relationships.

Illegal Firearm Possession

Various international agreements, including the Arms Trade Treaty and EU directives, focus on combating the illegal possession, carrying, trade, acquisition, and storage of firearms.

- The EU has adopted a Strategy against Illicit Firearms, Small Arms, and Light Weapons, aiming to reduce the number of illegally possessed firearms.
- The Republic of Serbia has a Strategy on Small Arms and Light Weapons Control, emphasizing efforts to reduce threats from illegal firearm possession and misuse.
- Serbia has implemented processes for firearm legalization, which have resulted in the surrender of illegal firearms, ammunition, and explosive ordnance.
- The Criminal Code prescribes penalties for illicit firearm production, possession, carrying, and trafficking, ranging from imprisonment to fines, depending on the offense.
- In 2018, there were 1,104 reports of these criminal offenses, with most cases leading to criminal charges.

Service Weapons: Understanding Regulations and Special Laws

The Law on Weapons and Ammunition is a general framework governing the acquisition, possession, and carrying of weapons. However, various specialized laws define who can carry and use weapons and for what specific purposes. Some of these laws and their corresponding bylaws provide detailed regulations concerning the possession, carrying, and use of service weapons. In contrast, others primarily address the authorization to carry weapons, referring to the Law on Weapons and Ammunition for additional conditions and requirements.

One key aspect is the Law on Police, which can be considered a systemic law because it outlines the actions taken by competent authorities before making decisions about acquiring, possessing, or carrying weapons. It includes procedures like security vetting.

Security Vetting Process

Security vetting is vital in determining whether certain security-related issues pose obstacles to acquiring specific rights, such as employment, obtaining permits for holding, carrying, or purchasing weapons, or enrolling in specific educational institutions.

Types of Laws Governing Service Weapons

Laws governing the carrying of service weapons can be categorized into three groups:

Laws Applying the Law on Weapons and Ammunition: Certain public sector employees, regulated by laws such as the Law on Game and Hunting and the Forest Law, are authorized to carry weapons. These laws align with the conditions specified in the Law on Weapons and Ammunition.

Laws Referring to the Law on Weapons and Ammunition but with Special Provisions: Laws like the Law on Detective Activity and the Law on Private Security rely significantly on the Law on Weapons and Ammunition. However, they also introduce unique requirements for individuals to carry weapons as part of their professional tasks.

Laws Governing Self-Protection Activities: These laws provide legal entities and entrepreneurs the opportunity to organize self-protection activities, allowing them to protect their property, facilities, and personnel. While these laws have lenient conditions for holding and carrying weapons, they still impose certain requirements.

Security-Related Restrictions: Restrictions for obtaining licenses to carry service weapons, as defined in the Law on Detective Activity and the Law on Private Security, include:

- Explicitly stated final prison sentences or recent convictions for specific offenses
- Imposed security measures or protective measures
- Demonstrated behavioral traits that pose a threat to individuals or public order and peace based on security vetting in the individual's place of residence, stay, or work

Notably, these laws do not consider convictions related to the prevention of domestic violence or protective measures under the Family Law as impediments to obtaining permits for carrying weapons. Moreover, convictions for specific criminal offenses are considered impediments only if they result in imprisonment, which leaves room for leniency in some instances.

Supervision and Enforcement

The Ministry of Interior supervises private security activities, with authorized police officers responsible for ensuring compliance with regulations governing the possession and carrying of private security weapons. They have the authority to conduct unannounced inspections and enforce compliance. Additionally, officers may refer licensed individuals to undergo medical examinations if there are doubts regarding their mental and physical fitness to carry out security-related tasks. These laws governing the carrying of service weapons are interconnected with the Law on Weapons and Ammunition. Some laws introduce special provisions, each with distinct requirements and security-related impediments. Adequate supervision ensures compliance with these regulations, contributing to the safe use of service weapons.

Review Questions

1. What percentage of women globally have experienced physical and sexual violence, and what is the most common form of such violence?
2. How does the presence of firearms in households impact the risk of violence escalation in the context of domestic violence?

3. What percentage of domestic violence-related murders involve firearms, and who are the primary victims?
4. What role does the "gun culture" play in perpetuating firearms-related issues, and what historical and societal factors contribute to it?
5. How do international frameworks address gender-based violence and firearms control, and what are their limitations?
6. What are some critical areas of improvement needed in Serbia's legal framework and regulations regarding firearm ownership?
7. What percentage of firearm owners in Serbia are men, and how does this gender disparity relate to firearm-related crimes?
8. How are laws and regulations related to firearms possession in Serbia influenced by the country's efforts to join the European Union?

Discussion Points

1. Discuss the role of firearms in gender-based violence and domestic violence and how this issue is interconnected with gender equality.
2. Explore the impact of the "gun culture" on firearms-related issues and how it can be addressed to promote safety and gender equality.
3. Examine the gender perspectives in international and national firearms control frameworks and consider ways to make these frameworks more gender-sensitive.
4. Discuss the challenges in enforcing firearm regulations, particularly regarding medical and psychological assessments, and how these challenges can be addressed.

CHAPTER TWO: SMALL ARMS CONTROL AND THE CHALLENGE OF ORGANIZED CRIME

Summary of Chapter Two

1. Illicit small arms and light weapons are associated with organized crime, posing a severe threat to international security. Addressing this issue requires comprehensive measures, including marking, tracing, and recordkeeping, strong national legislation, and criminal justice system improvements.

2. International cooperation and information-sharing are essential to combat criminal groups' access to weapons. The United Nations Convention against Transnational Organized Crime and its Firearms Protocol plays a vital role in addressing illicit firearm activities.

3. A holistic approach to addressing terrorism, illicit trafficking in small arms and light weapons, and other forms of organized crime is encouraged, leveraging expertise and information available on these crimes.

4. The relevance of small arms and light weapons extends across various aspects of international peace and security, such as human rights, counter-terrorism, organized crime, peacekeeping, and development.

5. The alignment of small arms control, women's rights, peace, and sustainable development is increasingly recognized as essential. Gender-responsive small arms programming can enhance effectiveness and

inclusivity.

6. Gender analysis is a fundamental tool for incorporating gender considerations into small-arms programming, addressing disparities among genders, and exploring the intersection of gender with other identity markers.

Organized Crime

Illicitly acquired or trafficked small arms and light weapons have garnered increasing attention from the international community due to their destabilizing impact, particularly in the context of organized crime. This type of trafficking, although taking on local variations, often plays a pivotal role in serious criminal activities. Addressing this challenge necessitates a multifaceted approach, including comprehensive marking, tracing, and recordkeeping, robust border controls, and the enactment of strong national legislation, including criminalization. Effective responses must also be developed within the criminal justice system. Criminal groups gaining access to weapons can not only generate revenue but also facilitate other criminal activities, such as trafficking in illicit materials and human beings.

International cooperation and information-sharing are vital to combating the threat of criminal groups acquiring weapons. In this context, the Security Council, through resolution 2482 (2019), urged Member States to consider establishing appropriate laws and mechanisms that encourage broad international cooperation. When enacting national laws, States should also consider provisions protecting witnesses and whistleblowers, which can incentivize information-sharing with law enforcement authorities.

Complete adherence to the United Nations Convention against Transnational Organized Crime and its Firearms Protocol is vital. These agreements include requirements for legislative measures and the criminalization of offenses related to illicit firearm manufacturing, marking, and trafficking. They also encompass preventive measures, security measures, regulatory controls, and international cooperation, including information exchange, all aimed at safeguarding the legal market and facilitating cohesive law enforcement and criminal justice responses to cases of illicit firearm activities.

A holistic approach to addressing terrorism, illicit trafficking in SALW, and other forms of organized severe crime is encouraged. Such an approach leverages expertise, tools, and information available on these crimes and encompasses all forms of trafficking, including in drugs and human beings. The Security Council, along with relevant committees and panels of experts, should continue to examine how illicit trafficking in SALW and organized crime can reinforce each other in certain regions.

The Security Council's agenda has expanded to encompass new threats to international peace and security, making existing threats increasingly complex. The relevance of SALW, along with their ammunition, is evident across the Council's agenda, both in country-specific discussions and in thematic deliberations. Integrating considerations regarding arms and ammunition more effectively could enhance the Council's ability to promote international peace and security. More than dealing with the SALW issue in isolation is required to address the gravity and complexity of its challenges. The adverse consequences of illicit SALW manifest in various contexts, spanning human rights, counter-terrorism, organized crime, peacekeeping, humanitarian assistance, socioeconomic development, refugees, internal displacement, gender, and children's rights.

The 2030 Agenda for Sustainable Development calls for a significant reduction in all forms of violence and related deaths, including stemming illicit arms flows. If the international community is to make meaningful progress, it is imperative to substantially reduce deaths related to SALW in both conflict and non-conflict situations.

Alignment of SALW, Women's Rights, Peace, and Sustainable Development

Over the past two decades, there has been a noticeable alignment of global priorities concerning small arms control, women's rights and peace, and sustainable development. This convergence necessitates a shift in thinking and a novel approach to project implementation for small arms control professionals, policymakers, and donor governments. A fundamental understanding now widely accepted is that significant reductions in armed violence cannot be achieved without the full and equitable involvement of individuals of all genders. Furthermore, recognizing the gender-related aspects of violence and insecurity is crucial. The challenge at present lies in translating these insights into practical program implementation. For example, disarmament initiatives must account for the gendered dynamics of arms acquisition, usage, and misuse in affected regions. Similarly, community-based violence reduction efforts must integrate the perspectives and contributions of individuals of all genders into their design. The benefits of enhancing the gender responsiveness of small arms programs are substantial, making them more effective and advancing gender equality.

Gender-responsive Small Arms Programming

Armed violence wreaks havoc in the lives of individuals of all genders. Whether it takes the form of intimate partner violence, gang-related violence, individual homicides or suicides, or occurs within armed conflicts, armed violence is one of the most destructive aspects of contemporary society. Moreover, it is a profoundly gendered phenomenon, impacting and affecting individuals of different genders in unique ways, often linked to societal assumptions and expectations regarding their roles.

Many United Nations Security Council resolutions (UNSCR) within the Women, Peace, and Security (WPS) Agenda make explicit references to the impact of arms, armed conflict, or sexual violence on women and development, emphasizing women's participation in small arms control. Similarly, the SDs of the 2030 Agenda for Sustainable Development address gender equality and arms control for sustainable development. However, national action plans for WPS and small arms controls often exist separately, with few linkages made between the two. Bridging this gap is essential for creating genuinely gender-responsive programming.

Gender-responsive programming enhances effectiveness, inclusivity, and sustainability by acknowledging the diverse experiences of all genders and ensuring that small arms programs do not overlook critical groups affected by or contributing to armed violence. It can also play a role in transforming the gender dynamics that underlie violence, promoting gender equality, and addressing both the effects and causes of violence.

Tools for Gender-responsive Small Arms Programming

Armed violence inflicts suffering on people of all genders. Whether it is intimate partner violence, gang or drug-related violence, individual homicides or suicides, or violence during armed conflicts, armed violence is one of the most destructive aspects of modern life. United Nations Security Council resolutions (UNSCR) within the WPS Agenda explicitly acknowledge the impact of arms, armed conflict, and sexual violence on women and development. Similarly, the SDGs emphasize the need for both gender equality and arms control for sustainable development. UNSCRs on small arms also advocate for women's meaningful participation in combatting illicit small arms trade and stress the importance of gender-informed data collection.

Furthermore, the Arms Trade Treaty requires exporting states to assess the risks of minor arms misuse for gender-based violence. Despite these intertwined agendas, national action plans for WPS and small arms control often remain isolated, failing to establish meaningful links between them. Bridging this gap is crucial for achieving truly gender-responsive programming. Gender responsiveness enhances program effectiveness, inclusivity, and sustainability by considering the unique experiences of all genders, ensuring that small arms programs address the needs of all affected groups. It can also contribute to transforming the underlying gender dynamics that fuel violence, thereby promoting gender equality and addressing both the effects and causes of violence.

Gender analysis stands as a fundamental tool in the incorporation of gender considerations into small-arms programming. It revolves around a detailed examination of the gender-related aspects of a particular issue, serving as the cornerstone for identifying components of gender-responsive small-arms programming. Gender analysis delves into understanding the disparities in the positions of individuals of different genders to one another. It explores their access to resources, opportunities, constraints, and power within a specific context. Importantly, gender analysis uncovers the underlying gender norms and their connections to weapons and armed violence.

Additionally, it explores the intersection of gender with other identity markers such as age, class, ethnicity, religion, sexual orientation, rural or urban location, disability, or marital status. This approach, known as intersectionality, adds depth to the analysis. Disaggregated data by sex and age will help inform small-arms programming that is gender-responsive.

The Normative and Legal Landscape of Small Arms Programming

The Women, Peace, and Security (WPS) Agenda

The WPS Agenda is grounded in the principle that integrating gender perspectives and women's rights can positively impact the lives of women, men, girls, and boys. While this applies to all aspects of women's lives, the WPS Agenda addresses how women are uniquely affected by violence and conflict, emphasizing their role in building and sustaining peace for the security of all individuals. By advocating for a gender perspective in peace and security, the WPS Agenda examines whether and how men and women are differently affected by specific situations or problems, thereby addressing women's distinct needs and capabilities. The WPS Agenda comprises four pillars:

participation (in peacebuilding and post-conflict resolution), prevention (of violence and rights violations), protection (from violence), and relief and recovery (creating the structural conditions for sustainable peace). The first three pillars are collectively known as the "three Ps."

Key Mechanisms

While the importance of women's experiences and capacities has been recognized for some time, their inclusion in high-level international policymaking is relatively recent. The adoption of UN Security Council Resolution (UNSCR) 1325, "Women, Peace and Security," in 2000 marked a significant milestone. Subsequently, eight other resolutions (UNSCRs 1820, 1888, 1889, 1960, 2106, 2122, 2242, and 2467) collectively form the core of the WPS Agenda.

Implementation

National Action Plans (NAPs) are the primary means of implementing and localizing UNSCR commitments. However, the scope and quality of activities described in these plans, as well as their implementation, vary widely. For instance, fewer than half of them allocate a budget for implementation, and many demonstrate inadequate analysis and consideration of the connection between disarmament, gender equality, and violence. Besides, there remains an imbalance in addressing the "three Ps." The protection of women and girls is often emphasized at the expense of violence and conflict prevention. Some feminist scholars argue that this pattern perpetuates the perception of women as vulnerable and in need of protection, rather than recognizing their agency. Others contend that the WPS Agenda has been co-opted to perpetuate militarism and violence rather than driving change and advancing peace as initially intended.

The 2030 Agenda for Sustainable Development

The 2030 Agenda represents a comprehensive and interconnected approach to sustainable socioeconomic development, building on earlier multilateral processes and agreements. The Eight Millennium Development Goals (MDGs), established in 2000, aimed to eradicate extreme poverty by 2015, but progress needed to be more balanced. Recognizing the need for a new global development framework, the Post-2015 Development Agenda was initiated in 2012. However, two SDGs are particularly pertinent to Gendered arms control.

SDG 5 aims to achieve gender equality and empower all women and girls. All targets under SDG 5 align with the WPS Agenda, with specific relevance to ending discrimination against women and girls and eliminating violence against them.

SDG 16 seeks to promote peaceful and inclusive societies for sustainable development, provide access to justice for all, and build effective, accountable, and inclusive institutions at all levels. A notable SDG 16 target calls for reducing illicit financial and arms flows and combatting organized crime, which has relevance for small arms control.

Each SDG has a set of targets, totaling 169, measured by specific indicators. The voluntary national reviews (VNRs) submitted by member states provide updates on progress toward SDG implementation, offering a transparent platform for assessment.

Synthesis of the Intruments of Arms and Gender Mainstreaming

The three agendas encompass various instruments, from UN Security Council resolutions to binding action plans and legal agreements. They all operate within the UN system and enjoy substantial political support. Some of these instruments have well-established platforms and institutions to facilitate and assess their implementation. However, across all three agendas, the level of implementation varies, both in terms of politically and legally binding aspects. These three frameworks share numerous points of convergence, which can lead to mutually beneficial outcomes. Enhancing this convergence is crucial for developing more effective and coherent policies and programs because the challenges addressed by these agendas are interconnected and complex. Two apparent areas of convergence at the international level are:

A Human-Centric View of Security: All three agendas aim to enhance human security and alleviate suffering. They challenge the traditional state-centric view of security by emphasizing equality and promoting human development through holistic approaches. This approach aligns with a feminist perspective of peace and security. For instance, the Women, Peace, and Security (WPS) Agenda adopts an integrated security approach, while the 2030 Agenda emphasizes people-centered goals and the principle of leaving no one behind. Similarly, the small arms control regime agreements explicitly focus on reducing human suffering caused by illicit arms trade, acknowledging its implications for poverty and underdevelopment. Human rights considerations are central to the Convention against Transnational Organized Crime and its Protocols.

Good Governance, Transparency and Oversight: These agendas also strive for improved governance, transparency, and oversight. Voluntary National Reviews (VNRs) under the 2030 Agenda aim to facilitate experience-sharing to accelerate implementation, while the Arms Trade Treaty (ATT) targets transparency in the arms trade to combat corruption. Transparency issues motivated the creation of the ATT and are reinforced by its reporting obligations.

Leveraging Data Within and Between Agendas: One noticeable area of convergence is how implementing small arms control instruments can contribute to achieving Sustainable Development Goal (SDG) Target 16.4 and Goal 16 more broadly. Additionally, the application of SDG indicators related to gender and violence reduction can support the WPS Agenda and small arms control efforts. Data collected through reporting requirements and practices of small arms control instruments can verify progress toward Target 16.4. For instance, Indicator 16.4.2 measures the proportion of seized arms with established illicit origins, with reporting practices from arms control agreements facilitating data collection for this indicator. Moreover, the use of sex-disaggregated data across agendas can lead to a better understanding of gender-differentiated impacts.

Gender Perspective in Security and Development: Another area of convergence is the integration of gender perspectives into security and development. The ATT explicitly addresses the risk of arms contributing to gender-based violence, connecting directly to SDG Target 5.2. It can also advance the prevention pillar of the WPS Agenda. While some tensions exist, such as large arms-producing countries struggling with assessing GBV risks in arms transfer decisions, there is an increasing recognition of the gendered impact of small arms. Recent progress, including gender mainstreaming and data collection efforts, demonstrates the potential for further alignment among these agendas.

Despite these convergences, there remains room for improving the integration of small arms control into the WPS Agenda and the explicit inclusion of gender considerations in SDG 16 to support women's roles in peace and recovery processes without co-opting the core values of the WPS Agenda.

Small Arms Control Regime

The international small arms control regime is a collection of global and regional agreements designed to address the proliferation, diversion, and misuse of small arms. It tackles both legal and illegal markets, aiming to reduce the human suffering caused by small arms and light weapons. The international small arms control regime comprises various mechanisms. However, the term "regime" here implies an informal set of guiding institutions and norms rather than a formal network of legal instruments. The core of this regime includes four key components:

The UN Program of Action to Prevent, Combat, and Eradicate the Illicit Trade in Small Arms and Light Weapons (PoA): This foundational normative agreement, established in 2001, provides a basis for international small arms control efforts. It features politically binding global commitments that mandate states to develop and implement practical measures to combat the illicit trade in small arms. These measures include improving national legislation, regulations, import/export controls, marking, tracing, stockpile management, and recordkeeping.

The UN Protocol against the Illicit Manufacturing of and Trafficking in Firearms, Their Parts and Components and Ammunition (Firearms Protocol): Adopted in 2001 and effective from 2005, this protocol is part of the UN Convention against Transnational Organized Crime. While it represents the first legally binding global instrument addressing small arms, its scope is narrower than the PoA. It primarily focuses on law enforcement, requiring state parties to criminalize illicit manufacturing and trade in firearms.

The International Tracing Instrument (ITI): Established in 2005 following a recommendation from the PoA, the ITI is a politically binding instrument that facilitates cooperation on tracing small arms. Its provisions cover areas such as marking, recordkeeping, cooperation in tracing, implementation, and follow-up activities.

The Arms Trade Treaty (ATT): Enacted in 2013, the ATT is a multilateral agreement that regulates international transfers of conventional arms, including small arms. It is renowned for integrating human rights and humanitarian concerns into global arms control. States parties to the ATT are obligated to assess the potential negative human and humanitarian impacts of prospective weapons transfers, as well as the potential for diversion to illicit markets, before granting export authorization.

All four arms control regimes have regular meeting cycles during which state parties or member states assess progress and, theoretically, strengthen or build upon the original instruments. The ATT has a secretariat, while the PoA and ITI are jointly considered through a shared implementation support system. In some regions and countries, national small arms focal points and commissions provide additional support and oversight for implementation and coordination, although the PoA does not mandate their existence. Reporting, a mechanism used to evaluate compliance and promote transparency, is mandatory for ATT state parties and voluntary under the PoA. Reporting is compulsory under the ITI and states parties to the Firearms

Protocol report their progress as part of their broader reporting under the Organized Crime Convention. In 2012, state parties established an open-ended intergovernmental Working Group on Firearms to advise and assist with implementation.

Additionally, several regional and sub-regional agreements on small arms control and transfers exist, particularly in Africa, Latin America, and Europe. Two United Nations Security Council Resolutions (UNSCRs 2117 and 2220) have been adopted on small arms in 2013 and 2015, respectively. The UN Human Rights Council has also passed resolutions on firearms and arms transfers. In 2017, the High Commissioner for Human Rights issued a report on arms transfers and human rights protection, and the UN General Assembly's First Committee annually adopts multiple small arms-related resolutions.

Extended Parties' involvement in the drive for Gender Perspectives in Arms Control

Until recently, gender perspectives within UN small arms conferences were mainly advocated by civil society groups, UN agencies, and entities focusing on women's empowerment or gender issues. These organizations promoted legally binding criteria related to gender-based violence (GBV) in the Arms Trade Treaty (ATT). They aimed to address the gender-related blind spots in the Program of Action (PoA). Local and national women's groups have also long sought to address the gender-related limitations of the PoA. In recent years, there has been a significant shift in this landscape. Sweden (2014) and Canada (2017) established feminist foreign and development assistance policies, while other countries like Ireland and Trinidad and Tobago have prioritized gender considerations in disarmament and arms control forums. This informal grouping of like-minded states has emerged, championing gender-related issues in the context of disarmament. Additionally, more non-governmental actors are engaging in these topics.

These developments highlight the growing recognition of the convergence between the Women, Peace, and Security (WPS) Agenda, small arms control, and the 2030 Agenda for Sustainable Development. Gender considerations, especially those related to Goal 5 of the 2030 Agenda, are gaining prominence within small arms control discussions. The key takeaways are as follows:

- There is increased interest and support for advancing gender perspectives in small arms control across governments, UN bodies, and non-governmental organizations.
- Convergence between these agendas is formally recognized within small arms control, but only with some opposition.

Obstacles to Future Progress

Despite progress, several challenges and knowledge gaps persist in advancing gender perspectives in small arms control:

"Add Women and Stir" Approach: Some discussions still conflate key concepts, equating gender perspectives with merely increasing women's participation or focusing on women's protection. This approach overlooks the broader aspects of gender and lacks precision and clarity in policies and documents.

Lack of Reciprocity: The convergence encouraged by the small arms control community is only sometimes reciprocated by those working solely in development or the Women, Peace, and Security (WPS) Agenda. Collaborative efforts across these agendas often occur more at national and regional levels than multilateral ones. The knowledge and experiences of the WPS community still need to be fully integrated into small arms control efforts. While progress has been made, addressing these challenges will be crucial in achieving meaningful results and fully leveraging the potential for convergence among these agendas.

Local to Global and Back Again

A pervasive challenge in multilateral frameworks is the disconnect between local experiences and global decision-making. The actual experiences of gender-based violence (GBV), gender discrimination, and poverty are often overlooked within UN conference settings. Simultaneously, translating decisions made at the UN and other international institutions into national legislation, policies, and public awareness is a complex and time-consuming process.

For instance, discussions within the Arms Trade Treaty (ATT) working groups have revealed a substantial gap between the diplomatic community's understanding of the Treaty's requirements concerning GBV and that of officials responsible for issuing licenses in national capitals. Moreover, limited input has been sought from Women, Peace, and Security (WPS) or gender experts in these discussions. In addressing this gap, civil society plays a crucial role by disseminating information, reminding states of their commitments, and bridging these knowledge gaps. Women-led grassroots civil society groups have effectively operationalized UNSCR 1325 beyond government actions. Civil society organizations working across these issues often struggle to influence UN discussions within security forums significantly. Constraints in terms of resources and limited opportunities for official contributions hinder their participation. Another challenge lies with the gaps between various ministries and departments. Commitments made in multilateral settings may need to be more effectively implemented, applied, or even understood by officials in different parts of government.

However, knowledge gaps persist, including issues related to key concepts and approaches. There is also a lack of equal and meaningful gender diversity, as well as an understanding of gender diversity versus women's participation. Other gaps include the following:

- Awareness of convergence with other agendas within the small arms control community may not be reciprocated by groups or networks exclusively focused on WPS or development.
- A gap exists between agreements and statements made in UN fora and their application at national levels or by other government officials and departments. Local perspectives and lived experiences of GBV are only sometimes well represented or integrated into diplomatic or UN-based discussions.

Thus, while progress has been made, challenges and knowledge gaps persist, including the need for more comprehensive gender analysis and better integration of local perspectives. There is also a need for increased engagement from the WPS and development communities in arms control issues, as well as a drive to overcome political opposition. However, the momentum for recognizing and acting on areas of convergence remains strong. Recent resolutions and initiatives reinforce these efforts, and upcoming anniversaries present further opportunities to deepen gains and ensure gender-responsive, practical, and effective programs and policies.

Review Questions

1. What role do illicit small arms and light weapons play in organized crime, and why is it essential to address this issue on an international level?
2. What are the critical components of the international small arms control regime, and how do they contribute to reducing human suffering caused by small arms?
3. How do international agreements like the United Nations Convention against Transnational Organized Crime and its Firearms Protocol address the issue of illicit minor arms trafficking?
4. Why is international cooperation and information-sharing crucial in combating criminal groups' access to weapons?
5. How does gender-responsive small arms programming enhance the effectiveness of efforts to control small arms, and why is it important to consider gender perspectives in this context?
6. What are the obstacles to advancing gender perspectives in small arms control, and how can these challenges be addressed?
7. How can the convergence of the Women, Peace, and Security (WPS) Agenda, small arms control, and the 2030 Agenda for Sustainable Development lead to mutually beneficial outcomes?
8. What are the key pillars of the Women, Peace, and Security (WPS) Agenda, and how do they relate to small arms control and gender considerations?

Discussion Points

1. The text highlights the importance of gender-responsive small arms programming. How can countries and international organizations better integrate gender considerations into their small arms control efforts?

2. The convergence of different international agendas, such as the WPS Agenda, small arms control, and sustainable development, is recognized as beneficial. What steps can be taken to strengthen this convergence and improve cooperation among these agendas?

3. The text discusses the challenges related to local-to-global and back-again dynamics in multilateral frameworks. How can international organizations bridge the gap between global decision-making and local experiences regarding minor arms issues?

4. Aligning small arms control with women's rights, peace, and sustainable development is crucial. How can civil society and non-governmental organizations play a more significant role in advancing these agendas at both national and international levels?

CHAPTER THREE: EMPOWERING GENDER EQUALITY: INTEGRATING A GENDER PERSPECTIVE IN SMALL ARMS CONTROL

Summary of Chapter Three

1. MOSAIC (Modular Small-Arms-Control Implementation Compendium) is a voluntary toolkit that helps combat the illicit trade and misuse of small arms and light weapons (SALW). It aligns with key global agreements and contributes to the Sustainable Development Goals, particularly Goal 16.

2. The development of MOSAIC involved a decade of coordinated efforts within the UN system, engaging 24 partner entities with expertise spanning various areas.

3. MOSAIC is accessible to governments and organizations aiming to enhance small-arms control efforts and reduce the risk of these weapons falling into the wrong hands.

4. Gender equality and reducing illicit arms flows are intrinsically connected through the Sustainable Development Goals, and addressing the gender perspective in SALW control is crucial.

5. Gender mainstreaming ensures that the consequences of SALW control initiatives on men and women are considered at all stages, facilitating

a deeper understanding of their roles in conflict and post-conflict situations.

6. Small arms have disparate impacts on men and women, and addressing the link between masculinity, small arms, and violence is vital for long-term strategies to reduce violence.

MOSAIC and Arms Control

Modular Small-Arms-Control Implementation Compendium (MOSAIC) embodies the practical realization of key global agreements designed to combat the illicit trade, accumulation, and misuse of SALW. These agreements include:

- The Program of Action on the illicit trade in SALW.
- The International Tracing Instrument.
- The Firearms Protocol supplements the UN Convention against Transnational Organized Crime.
- The Arms Trade Treaty.

MOSAIC modules are grounded in best practices, codes of conduct, and standard operating procedures developed at regional and sub-regional levels. These guidelines have been crafted by the UN, benefiting from expert input worldwide. Importantly, MOSAIC is an entirely voluntary toolkit. MOSAIC contributes to achieving the Sustainable Development Goals, particularly Goal 16, which focuses on promoting peaceful, just, and inclusive societies, and its indicator 16.4, which calls for a significant reduction in illicit arms flows.

Who developed MOSAIC?

Governments often turn to the UN for advice and support on issues related to SALW control, encompassing legislative, programmatic, and operational aspects. UN agencies recognized the need to provide consistent, high-quality advice and support across the UN system, similar to established standards in other areas such as mine action, disarmament, and ammunition management. The development of MOSAIC involved a decade of coordinated efforts within the UN system. It engaged 24 partner entities with expertise spanning development, weapons management, gender, public health, and more. An external expert reference group comprising over 300 specialists, including representatives from NGOs and industry, played a crucial role in shaping each module.

Who can use MOSAIC?

MOSAIC is accessible to any government or organization seeking to enhance small-arms control efforts. Implementing small-arms control initiatives in alignment with MOSAIC modules reduces the risk of weapons falling into the wrong hands, be it criminals, armed groups, terrorists, or other malevolent actors.

Achieving Gender Equality and Reducing Illicit Arms Flows

The international community, through the SDGs, has committed to goals such as achieving gender equality (Goal 5) and significantly reducing illicit arms flows and violent deaths (Goal 16). These goals are intrinsically connected. Addressing the illicit trade in small arms and light weapons in all aspects and countering the misuse of legally and illegally owned firearms necessitates attention to the human factors influencing the supply, demand, and misuse of these weapons across all levels of society. It also requires mobilizing and building the capacity of all stakeholders and institutions capable of contributing to comprehensive solutions.

Applying a gender perspective to the uncontrolled proliferation and misuse of small arms recognizes that these weapons have disparate impacts on men and women, and both genders have equal rights to engage in efforts to control them. Gender mainstreaming, as a practice, ensures that the consequences of SALW control initiatives on both men and women are considered at all stages: assessment, planning, implementation, monitoring, and evaluation.

Gender mainstreaming facilitates a deeper understanding of the roles men and women play concerning SALW, whether during conflict, post-conflict reconstruction, or peacetime.

Promoting gender-balanced participation in SALW control safeguards the rights of both men and women to partake in decision-making regarding an issue that affects everyone's security. Achieving equal participation by women necessitates a concerted focus on their inclusion, especially women from affected communities and civil society, along with a commitment to gender-sensitive monitoring and evaluation. The integration of gender perspectives into SALW control processes, as mandated by international instruments, enhances comprehension of the factors driving demand for and misuse of these weapons. It also highlights their impact on human rights, development, and security. Gender mainstreaming facilitates the development of holistic, targeted, and effective responses.

The Gendered Nature of SALW

The gendered dimensions of the uncontrolled proliferation and misuse of SALW, as well as gender-related aspects of SALW control, are incorporated into all modules of the Modular Small-arms-control Implementation Compendium (MOSAIC). This document consolidates the gender-related content from other MOSAIC modules, establishes principles, and offers guidance on implementing gender-responsive SALW control programs. The MOSAIC aims to assist practitioners in designing, implementing, monitoring, and evaluating SALW control initiatives, whether they involve legislation, policy, programming, or projects. The document provides advice on gender-sensitive interventions and actions to ensure the fairness and effectiveness of these initiatives. Issues related to gender in the context of disarmament, demobilization, and reintegration of ex-combatants are addressed in the Integrated Disarmament, Demobilization, and Reintegration Standards (IDDRS 5.10, Women, Gender, and DDR). Similarly, matters related to SALW control concerning boys and girls are discussed in MOSAIC 06.20, Children, Adolescents, Youth, and Small Arms and Light Weapons.

Effects of Misuse of SALW

Every year, over half a million people worldwide lose their lives to violence, both in conflict zones and elsewhere. Small arms are involved in nearly half of all violent deaths globally, including roughly one-third of killings of women and girls, which is often referred to as femicide. Available evidence indicates that 84 percent of the victims are male, and only 16 percent are female. While men make up the majority of victims in high-violence countries, it is essential to note that women face the highest risk of being killed in these settings. The presence of minor arms-related violence significantly increases the risk for everyone, regardless of gender. Whether as perpetrators, victims, or witnesses of armed violence, individuals, regardless of their gender, can suffer severe and long-lasting psychological trauma.

Effects on Men and Boys

Most direct victims of minor arms violence are male, with young men aged 15-29 being particularly vulnerable. They not only represent the primary victims of violence in general but also account for a more significant proportion of victims of minor arms violence. Young men are also more likely to use small arms when involved in criminal activities compared to other demographic groups.

Violent Masculinity

Young men actively engage with and internalize social norms related to masculinity, shaping their behavior and attitudes. A young man's gender is not the sole factor determining their association with or inclination toward armed violence; instead, their understanding of societal and cultural ideals of masculinity plays a crucial role in whether they turn to armed violence. The connection between masculinity, minor arms possession, and violent behavior is socially constructed. Young boys from childhood are often more exposed to toy guns or create makeshift ones, imitating characters seen in violent media or real-life gangs and militias. Small arms may also be linked to rituals marking the transition from boyhood to manhood. Calls to take up arms often appeal to conventional notions of manliness.

Women's attitudes can also contribute to the cultural conditioning equating masculinity with violence and small arms ownership and use. Women sometimes overtly encourage men to engage in conflict or shame them for not doing so. More subtly, they support attitudes and stereotypes that reinforce this association. While controlling the availability and regulation of small arms is crucial in curbing armed violence, these measures alone will not address the underlying demand factors. Tackling the deeply ingrained link between masculinity, small arms, power, and violent behavior that drive violent behavior will help to deal with the deeper causes that drive the demand for and misuse of small arms by men. Countering these socially constructed yet enduring associations is a vital component of practical, long-term strategies to reduce violence. Addressing the issue of violent masculinity requires a solid commitment to gender equality and redefining manhood to exclude aggression and violence.

Men/Boys as Possible Victims of Sexual and Gender-Based Violence

Although women and girls primarily fall victim to gender-based and sexual violence, these forms of violence can also be directed against men and boys, especially during armed conflicts, often exacerbated by the use of small arms. Non-combatant men may face gender-based violence, including forced conscription, sexual violence, and sex-selective massacres. Reports of sexual violence against men and boys have emerged in numerous armed conflicts during the early 21st century. Moreover, the presence of small arms may increase the risk of male suicide, as it is mainly men who use small arms for self-inflicted harm. Most suicides involving small arms occur in homes, with the individuals often having alcohol in their system and no prior contact with psychiatric services or a history of self-harm.

Effects on Women and Girls

Women and girls are disproportionately affected by small arms in several ways. Despite their lower ownership and use of small arms, they face a higher rate of death by gunshot due to the higher number of men killed with these weapons. The fact that nearly all small arms are owned, used, and misused by men makes women particularly vulnerable. Small arms play a significant role in lethal violence in general and violence against women in particular. The brandishing of small arms for intimidation, threats, or coercion often precedes their actual use. Women who fall victim to femicide, the killing of women because of their gender, have often reported prior threats involving small arms as part of a pattern of coercive violence perpetrated by their male partners.

Femicide

Regions with high femicide rates also tend to have high overall rates of lethal violence. However, in non-conflict settings, where most violent deaths occur, the proportion of female victims tends to be lower in countries with high rates of violent death and higher in countries with low rates. This finding reflects the fact that in countries with high violent death rates, the majority of victims are men, while in low-violence countries, women make up a more significant proportion of victims. In countries with high femicide rates, more than half of killings of women and girls involve small arms. Most perpetrators of femicide are male, often current or former intimate partners, family members, or friends of the victim.

Intimate Partner and Domestic/Family-Related Violence

Intimate partner and domestic/family-related violence, predominantly targeting women, is a universal and highly gendered issue. Most victims of such violence are women subjected to coercive, controlling violence, which can involve the use of small arms. The proportion of intimate partner and family-related violence, relative to all femicides, varies between countries.

Small Arms in the Home

The presence of small arms in households increases the risk to all members, especially women, as these weapons can be used to threaten or cause harm. Small arms represent a hazardous object in homes, posing a particular risk to children and increasing the likelihood of fatal injuries. Small arms are also often used in suicides, and they can pose a greater risk to women and children when brought home by male soldiers or police officers suffering from post-traumatic stress. Work-related small arms, both inside and outside the home, contribute to the normalization of small arms in public and private spaces, leading to societal militarization with potential negative consequences for women.

Generally, easy access to small arms is linked to gender-based and sexual violence, primarily affecting women and girls. Refugees from armed conflicts often cite rape as a primary reason for fleeing their homes, with armed men being the primary perpetrators. Some forms of sexual violence during conflicts, such as rape, can amount to war crimes and may constitute elements of genocide. Indicators of minor arms-related sexual violence include armed individuals conducting house raids, ex-militias absconding with their small arms after integration into armed forces, arms bearers infiltrating refugee camps, mass displacement due to insecurity, increased fear among women and girls, and reports of girls disappearing while traveling to or from school in areas with arms bearers.

Indirect Effects of Armed Conflict and Violence

Non-combatants, regardless of gender or age, suffer significantly from the indirect consequences of armed conflict, including reduced access to essential resources and services. Women and girls are significantly affected, facing death and disability due to pregnancy and childbirth complications, as well as the spread of sexually transmitted diseases through rape. They also endure various forms of GBV as a result of small arms availability and misuse. Women are disproportionately impacted by the social and economic effects of armed conflict, as they often assume increased responsibilities when male family members are involved in conflict. The burden of supporting families falls on women when male relatives are killed, injured, or disabled, leaving them more vulnerable to gender based violence. Displaced populations, mainly consisting of women, children, and seniors, face significant challenges and risks due to ongoing violence and high numbers of weapons within these communities. Post-conflict communities may also feel compelled to arm themselves due to ongoing insecurity.

Mainstreaming Gender in Small Arms Control

Integrating gender perspectives into small arms control initiatives at the legislative, policy, program, or project level significantly enhances their effectiveness in addressing the adverse impacts of small arms and light weapons misuse. Ensuring gender is considered throughout all stages of such initiatives is essential for their overall quality.

Engage Early with Expertise in Gender: Gender equality organizations, women's groups, and gender specialists should be engaged from the outset of small arms control initiatives, spanning assessment, strategy development, program design, implementation, and evaluation.

Build Consensus Among Stakeholders: Establishing a shared understanding of gender's crucial role in small arms control and its diverse impacts on women and men is fundamental to integrating gender perspectives effectively. Stakeholders should commit to gender-sensitive approaches, including gender-sensitivity training and long-term mentoring, as needed. Incorporating a formal statement supporting gender equality within project/program documents, along with a clear plan for gender-sensitive approaches, can demonstrate this commitment. In settings resistant to gender perspectives, framing gender-sensitive approaches within a broader human security and human rights framework may be helpful.

Collect and Use Sex- and Age-Disaggregated Data: Collecting data that is disaggregated by sex and age is essential for understanding the gender-specific impacts of minor arms misuse and designing gender-responsive interventions. Accurate information is crucial for ensuring that small arms control interventions address the unique security needs of women and men.

Conduct a Gender Analysis: Gender analysis is the foundation for mainstreaming gender into small-arms control initiatives. It assesses the connections between gender relations and small-arms misuse, revealing inequalities and guiding gender-responsive interventions. Without gender analysis, small arms control initiatives may inadvertently reinforce existing gender inequalities.

Address Identified Gender Patterns: Gender analysis, based on sex- and age-disaggregated data, should uncover specific gender patterns related to small arms use, misuse, effects, and barriers to women's participation. Initiatives should take concrete steps to address these identified gender patterns.

Support the Meaningful Participation of Women: Women should be actively involved at all levels of small arms control initiatives, including policymaking, planning, implementation, monitoring, and evaluation. Achieving gender balance within national coordinating mechanisms for small arms and light weapons control is crucial.

Track Progress Using Gender-Sensitive Indicators: Monitoring and evaluating small arms control initiatives should ensure that gender-specific risks are addressed equitably, that both men and women participate meaningfully, and that benefits are shared equally. Indicators used for monitoring and evaluation should be disaggregated by sex to detect and rectify gender imbalances.

Gender-Responsive Approach to SALW Control

Effective gender-responsive SALW control should encompass the following key components:

- The commitment of the stakeholders to programs that adhere to global and regional agreements on SALW control, precisely those elements designed to promote gender equality and empower women.
- Emphasis on local ownership at all levels.
- Support from donors.
- Establishment of coordination mechanisms that ensure the active partici-

pation of women and women's organizations. This aligns with MOSAIC 03.40, "National Coordinating Mechanisms on Small Arms and Light Weapons Control," as well as UN Security Council Resolutions 1325 (2000) and 1899 (2009).

- Integration of gender-sensitive baseline assessments and program design.
- Gender training for government officials, service providers, media, and civil society.
- Development of gender-responsive budgets.
- Utilization of gender expertise, including contributions from gender specialists, female leaders, representatives of women's groups, and men working to combat gender-based violence.
- Provision of appropriate services to both women and men.

Integration into Regional and National Policy Development

National action plans concerning SALW control (refer to MOSAIC 04.10) should be integrated into broader national development strategies, poverty reduction efforts, peacebuilding initiatives, and human security frameworks. Gender and age sensitivity should be mainstreamed throughout these policies.

Regional and national policy development processes for small arms and light weapons control should draw on gender expertise, as mentioned in Clause 7.2. Consultation with gender specialists, both female and male, and with women's and men's groups dedicated to combating gender-based violence should inform these processes.

These policy development processes should ensure a balanced representation of women and men in the teams responsible for assessing, drafting, implementing, monitoring, and evaluating small arms and light weapons control efforts.

National Coordinating Mechanisms

Comprehensive guidance on national coordinating mechanisms for SALW control is provided in MOSAIC 03.40. These mechanisms should promote gender balance, women's participation, and leadership. They should include:

- The government ministry that is responsible for women's affairs.
- Civil society organizations, particularly women's groups and men's groups, are working to eradicate gender-based violence, either as invited experts or through public consultation.
- The domestic/family violence unit of the police force, if it exists.
- Female parliamentarians.

Addressing Human Trafficking

Trafficking in SALW often intersects with other forms of trafficking, including human trafficking. Women, girls, and young boys are often the majority of human trafficking victims, and traffickers may use women as smuggling agents. Addressing human trafficking in the context of addressing the illicit trade in SALW requires the following:

- Consider the interconnectedness of various forms of trafficking and establish cooperation between relevant sectors and states.
- Develop collaboration, consultation, and engagement with social and economic development sectors, as well as civil society organizations, to address the needs of those drawn into trafficking networks as a survival strategy.
- Explore targeted income-generating programs as practical tools for preventing arms smuggling.
- Utilize testimonies of trafficked individuals, anecdotal evidence, and qualitative data when formulating anti-trafficking policies and action plans.
- Encourage collaboration with women's organizations, particularly those with expertise in designing and implementing community-level trafficking prevention and victim assistance programs.
- Provide training for male and female border control personnel, especially border police and customs officers, to identify and interview victims of

human trafficking. Civil society organizations specializing in gender issues may assist with such training.

Weapons Collection and Destruction

During weapons collection programs, women can play a vital role in convincing their partners, children, and family members to relinquish small arms or may hand them in on behalf of relatives who fear legal consequences. Therefore, it is essential to plan for and encourage the participation of women in weapons surrender.

- Consult with local women when planning the collection of small arms and light weapons to gather valuable information on the prevalence of weapons and security considerations.
- Consider the opinions, roles, and needs of local women when designing incentives to boost participation in the collection process.
- Develop information and awareness campaigns on weapons collection that include strategies targeting women's participation.
- Address factors related to dominant norms of masculinity that fuel the demand for small arms among men, particularly young men.
- Prioritize employment opportunities and other incentives related to weapons collection for women, especially those who have survived minor arms-related violence, lost family members to such violence, or care for survivors of such violence. These women may still have small arms or light weapons in their households used by their deceased or injured male relatives.
- Encourage civil society organizations promoting gender equality and women's empowerment to:
- Run awareness campaigns supporting voluntary weapons collection programs, focusing on women, youth, and other civil society groups.
- Participate in weapons collection as intermediaries between communities and state security officials.
- Provide public information on weapons amnesties and incentives for

turning in weapons and raise awareness to boost collection campaigns.

- Enhance confidence in weapons destruction processes by raising awareness about their benefits and participating in and officially monitoring public destruction events.

International Small Arms Transfers

MOSAIC 03.20 and 03.21 offer gender-sensitive guidance on national controls over international small arms and light weapons transfer and the end-use of such weapons, respectively. When evaluating requests for export authorizations of small arms or light weapons:

- Take into account the risk that these weapons may be used to commit or facilitate serious acts of gender-based violence or violence against women and children. If a significant risk is identified, the export should not be authorized.
- If, after granting an authorization, an exporting state becomes aware of new relevant information related to the violations mentioned in the previous point, reassess the export authorization after appropriate consultations with the importing state.

Review Questions

1. What are the critical global agreements that MOSAIC aligns with to control small arms and light weapons?
2. Who were the main contributors and partners involved in the development of MOSAIC?
3. Who can access and use MOSAIC to enhance small arms control efforts?
4. How are gender equality and reducing illicit arms flows interconnected through the Sustainable Development Goals?
5. What is gender mainstreaming, and why is it essential in the context of small-arms control?
6. What are the effects of using small arms on men and boys?

7. How does the association between masculinity, small arms, and violence manifest?

8. How are women and girls disproportionately affected by small arms, and what role do these weapons play in femicide?

Discussion Points

1. Discuss the significance of integrating a gender perspective into small-arms control efforts. How does considering gender at all stages of initiatives contribute to more effective solutions?

2. Explore the potential strategies for addressing the deeply ingrained link between masculinity, small arms, power, and violent behavior. How can societies redefine manhood to exclude aggression and violence?

3. What roles can women and men play in promoting gender-balanced participation in SALW control? How can their involvement contribute to more inclusive and effective decision-making?

4. Consider the impact of small arms on different aspects of society, including domestic violence, suicide, and economic consequences. How can these impacts be addressed in small-arms control initiatives?

CHAPTER FOUR: THE IMPACT OF SMALL ARMS ON GENDER ROLES AND VIOLENCE IN CONFLICT ZONES

Summary of Chapter Four

1. Types of Weapons Collection Programs: Various voluntary weapons collection programs, including buy-backs, amnesty periods, exchange programs, and collective development initiatives, have been implemented to reduce the presence of small arms and light weapons (SALW) in conflict zones.

2. Collaborative Effort for Weapons Collection: Successful weapons collection programs often involve collaboration between international organizations, governments, and civil society groups to address the challenges of collecting and managing weapons.

3. Gender-Related Consequences of Cross-Border Conflicts in Africa: Cross-border conflicts in Africa have led to an increase in gender-based violence, with SALW playing a significant role in exacerbating violence, both during and after conflicts.

4. Disruption of Traditional Gender Roles by Small Arms: The easy accessibility of small and lightweight firearms has disrupted traditional gender roles in conflict zones, enabling women and children to engage in combat and eroding cultural norms.

5. Gender Differences in Attitudes towards SALW: While there is a percep-

tion that women dislike firearms and men favor them, limited research has explored these gender-related attitudes toward SALW.

6. The Need for Practical Strategies: Gender-aware policies, research, and activism are required to address the impact of SALW on gender-specific violence and social norms.

Weapon Collection Programs

There exist various types of weapons collection programs, including buy-backs, amnesty periods, weapons for development, lottery prizes, cash exchanges, vouchers for food and goods, scholarships, computers or radios, tools for trade and agriculture, housing and construction materials, infrastructure projects, and public health services. The primary categories of voluntary weapons collection programs are as follows:

Buy-Back Programs: These involve collecting weapons in exchange for cash, often at the black-market price or the average price of a legal sale. The process typically includes setting prices, specifying the types of guns to be collected, defining a time limit, and identifying collection points. In Nicaragua, a government-initiated gun buy-back program encouraged combatants not to re-arm, offering money, food, and micro-enterprise opportunities in exchange for weapons. This effort resulted in the destruction of 142,000 weapons between 1991 and 1993. In Haiti, the US Army conducted a buy-back program during its stability operation in the early 1990s, providing cash and a "no questions asked" policy to participants and collecting 33,000 weapons in 1994 and 1995.

Exchange Programs: In response to concerns that offering cash incentives could increase the value and demand for weapons, exchange programs have been developed, offering goods in return for surrendered weapons. In El Salvador, civil society, the business community, and the Catholic Church initiated the Goods for Guns program, conducting 23 voluntary weapons collection projects with international, government, and private funding.

Although it collected only 8 percent of the arms legally imported during that period, it raised public awareness. In Mozambique, the Christian Council of Churches ran the Tools for Arms program from 1995 to 2000, collecting weapons in exchange for various tools and machinery. The confiscated weapons were often transformed into public art and practical objects, contributing to peace advocacy.

Amnesty Programs: Some weapons collection programs offer amnesty to incentivize individuals to turn in their weapons. In Bosnia and Herzegovina, NATO's Stabilization Force conducted an ongoing weapons collection program (Operation Harvest) that guarantees anonymity and amnesty for those surrendering their guns. In 2000, this program collected 5,081 small arms, destroyed 2,642 landmines, and gathered 2.7 million rounds of 20mm ammunition.

Collective Development Programs: Also known as Weapons for Development, these initiatives have emerged in response to calls for incentives, such as infrastructure projects, that benefit entire communities rather than just individuals who possess weapons. This model aims to avoid rewarding armed individuals, engage non-combatants, and address collective demand factors. In Albania, the United Nations Development Program (UNDP) initiated the Gramsh Pilot Project, collecting 7,000 weapons and funding 12 development projects in one district from 1998 to 2000. UNDP expanded this model with the Weapons in Exchange for Development project from 2000–2002, collecting 6,000 weapons and supporting 23 projects in two districts. More recently, UNDP conducted the Weapons in Competition for Development project in all 36 districts of Albania, where communities competed for small infrastructure and development projects by turning in SALW. This effort resulted in the collection of 11,864 weapons and the awarding of 46 development projects in 5 districts.

International organizations that fund and support weapons collection programs include the UN and multilateral and bilateral agencies. The UN's Group of Interested States in Practical Disarmament Measures, composed of approximately 40 member countries, is mandated by the General Assembly to provide funding for practical disarmament programs at the national and local levels. Additionally, the UN Trust Fund for the Consolidation of Peace through Practical Disarmament Measures, administered by the UN Department for Disarmament Affairs, supports similar projects. UNDP, since 1999, has invested approximately $10 million in disarmament efforts. The World Bank's Post-Conflict Fund also backs disarmament programs worldwide, including demining efforts.

Collaborative Effort for Weapons Collection

In many instances, international organizations, national and local governments, and civil society groups collaborate to ensure the success of weapons collection programs. For example, in Macedonia, the parliament established an agency to manage the program, with civil society's assistance in launching a nationwide public awareness campaign. Local and national government leaders oversaw the collection process at designated points, and UNDP incentivized participation by offering lottery tickets for various prizes. Over 45 days, nearly 6,000 weapons were collected. Weapons collection programs come with numerous challenges. Policymakers and practitioners have identified several important lessons:

Prior Assessment: It is crucial to assess the starting point, namely the number of existing weapons, to measure the program's impact.

Coherence: To prevent conflicting priorities, objectives, process plans, and target actors among involved parties, clear objectives, and transparency must be maintained throughout the process.

Incentives and Sanctions: Deciding whether to provide incentives or penalties—and determining their nature—can be a significant challenge. There is concern that offering rewards for arms may increase their value and demand, leading to other issues.

Combination with Other Efforts: Effective weapons collection programs must be part of a comprehensive peace and stability framework.

Gender-Related Consequences of Cross-Border Conflicts in Africa

In recent decades, Africa has experienced a surge in internal conflicts involving diverse ethnic, religious, or political factions within a single nation. Some of these conflicts spill over into cross-border clashes, engulfing an increasing number of civilians, some displaced within their own country, living in unsafe conditions, or forced to flee their homeland altogether. These conflicts have significant gender-related consequences. Gender-based violence not only escalates in public spaces but also permeates homes as traumatized individuals, often demobilized from combat, continue to perpetrate violence, redirecting their pain and anger toward those closest to them. South Africa, for instance, grapples with rising domestic violence and child abuse, making it challenging to declare the nation at peace.

The proliferation of SALW, owing to their widespread availability, mobility, and ease of use, plays a central role in wartime conflicts and contributes to social disarray, instability, insecurity, and crime long after conflicts have ended. One approach to mitigate their impact is to enhance our comprehension of how these prolific small weapons reinforce and sustain gender-specific expressions of violence before, during, and after conflicts.

Disruption of Traditional Gender Roles by Small Arms

The widespread forced displacement of civilians during large-scale conflicts has caused unprecedented social disruption. Modern warfare has expanded to affect civilian spaces where women, children, and seniors reside. Even traditional symbols of neutrality or vulnerability, such as waving a white flag or seeking refuge in places like churches, no longer guarantee safety. Schools are no longer sanctuaries as girls and boys are routinely abducted to join irregular armed groups. At the same time, women face robbery, rape, or abduction while working in fields or marketplaces. In contemporary African conflicts, many firearms in circulation are lightweight, easy to use, and durable, allowing armed women and children to engage in combat with the same ease and proficiency as men. Some warlords intentionally employ women and children as fighters to exploit the shock factor of being attacked by individuals perceived as "vulnerable." This strategy erodes cultural norms of care and protection, leaving lasting psychological scars. Contemporary wars have, thus, precipitated widespread destabilization of social and cultural norms regarding warfare. Notably, the way modern armed conflicts are waged, due to the easy accessibility of small weapons, has impacted traditions that reinforce gender power dynamics and contribute to the formation of male and female identities.

Gender Differences in Attitudes towards SALW

Traditionally, women are perceived as disliking firearms, while men are seen as favoring them. Although few formal studies have been conducted on this issue, anecdotal evidence suggests that women, men, and children do not have equal access to SALW and are differently affected by their misuse, both during and after conflicts. There is an ongoing debate about whether women, men, and children possess distinct attitudes regarding the widespread presence of firearms. Given the far-reaching consequences of minor arms misuse, it is crucial to document diverse perspectives to devise effective strategies for improving human security by curtailing the proliferation of millions of small arms in circulation.

SALW and the 'Continuum of Violence'

One characteristic of warfare, which often persists in the post-conflict phase, is the violent disruption of political, social, and cultural traditions. This destruction of values has specific implications for gender relations. Small arms significantly contribute to this process of social destruction, and their continued presence profoundly shapes post-conflict societal reconstruction. However, international attention has focused mainly on the source and legality of these weapons, neglecting the political dimensions of the small arms trade. Additionally, there has been a tendency to frame the small arms problem as stemming from 'illicit' or 'criminal' activities, which does not facilitate meaningful actions to address the effects of these weapons and the structural violence they perpetuate.

From a gender perspective, it is long overdue to shift the focus to the impact of SALW, whether legally owned and subject to gun laws or not. Gender researchers reject the fragmented understanding of violence, emphasizing that violence is not solely a private or individual issue but is socially and structurally produced by political systems that maintain male dominance through aggression. Gender researchers stress the importance of not exclusively concentrating on high levels of political violence during or after conflicts or the technical challenges of weapons proliferation but also acknowledging other forms of violence, such as domestic abuse, often socially sanctioned, predating wars, and continuing during peacetime.

Most wars do not aim for social transformation; therefore, it is unrealistic to expect people to change after a conflict ends suddenly. Those who believe violence is an appropriate response to conflict or stress are likely to carry that attitude forward, especially when societal traditions do not promote peace. Consequently, women often bear the brunt of social breakdown resulting from post-conflict violence. South Africa serves as a prime example, where women continue to experience severe abuse long after the official cessation of war. The easy availability of guns, lax gun control, and social acceptance of gun ownership all contribute to women's insecurity in post-war settings.

Hence, gender-aware research on the effects of small arms proliferation is crucial. Such research can help trace the links between 'everyday' violence and the 'unspeakable' extremes of violence seen in conflict situations. These links are, to a large extent, supported by gender ideologies that uphold and glorify male superiority while condoning male aggression toward women and children. Gender-aware peace researchers challenge these ideologies in all societies, whether caught up in violent conflict or ostensibly at peace. Attitudes like those that condone violence against women can only be overcome through activism grounded in well-documented evidence of how firearms impact women's lives. Accurate statistics are crucial for developing comprehensive legislation. South Africa is an excellent example of how, long after a war has officially come to an end, women can continue to suffer terrible abuse.

Guns are hazardous when they are kept at home, debunking popular myths about the protective power of firearms in violent societies. In some cases, men who kill their female partners are not considered to have committed an unthinkable act. Instead, others can understand, if not forgive, the notion that a man might be provoked to murder his female partner, especially if infidelity is suspected. Such attitudes, even among legal authorities, result in lenient sentences and contribute to the perpetuation of violence against women, thus underscoring the need for gender-aware research on the impact of small arms proliferation, as it can help elucidate the complex dynamics at play and inform policy and legal reforms.

SALW and Women's Attitudes

Globally, although more men than women die due to firearms, the easy availability of SALW perpetuates male dominance and facilitates violence against women in conflict zones. However, it is unproductive to depict women solely as victims and men solely as perpetrators. Instead, it is essential to analyze the intricate ways in which the widespread presence of guns and other light weapons reinforces ideologies of masculinity and femininity. In many societies, bearing arms carries significant cultural significance, intertwined with social rituals like a young man's rite of passage. Women in such societies are expected to support men's right to bear arms, but few observers have commented on the crucial role women play in normalizing gun ownership. In some societies, women actively encourage men to use arms in activities such as raids, believing that their success improves the family's economic position. In countries like South Africa, women may uphold the belief that their male partners need guns for protection. Such attitudes reveal that women cannot always be characterized as inherently peace-loving and fundamentally opposed to the presence and use of arms.

The Need for Practical Strategies

While the rhetoric of 'gender mainstreaming' has permeated international agreements, practical strategies to ensure equal attention to women and men have been challenging to implement. The proliferation of small arms and light weapons, their ease of use, and their lethal impact necessitate gender-aware policies, research, and activism. International agreements like the Beijing Platform of Action, the Windhoek Declaration, and Resolution 1325 provide formal avenues to hold governments and international agencies accountable for addressing gender-based violence perpetuated by small arms. However, these documents lack power if there is no political will to prioritize gender differences in addressing SALW.

It is essential to put more significant commitment to collecting sex-disaggregated data on the effects of small arms is essential as the first step in challenging the indifference and denial surrounding GBV facilitated by guns. Civil society organizations involved in gun control should develop awareness-raising and training models to establish a new culture of data collection. Standardizing data collection, especially regarding the sex of victims and perpetrators of firearm violence, is crucial to addressing the problem effectively. Such information will contribute to understanding how easily accessible guns are particularly perilous to women, limiting their choices and freedom and denying them the right to lead safe and fulfilling lives. It will also shed light on how dangerous notions of masculinity persist in violent societies, reinforcing the importance of ongoing activism to encourage positive expressions of male identity. Gender-aware research on the implications of small arms proliferation and disarmament is essential to comprehending the multifaceted impact of SALW on society. It helps uncover the complex roles women play concerning these weapons and contributes to efforts aimed at reducing their harmful consequences.

Peace Education, Community Participation, and Awareness-Raising

It is necessary to prioritize initiatives for SALW control related to peace education, community participation, risk education, and awareness-raising. The key points to note in that regard include the following:

- Consider the gendered impacts of small arms ownership, proliferation, and misuse.
- Integrate sex- and age-disaggregated data and gender analysis into assessments.
- Address the diverse needs and roles of women, men, girls, and boys in each context.
- Have a good understanding of the different roles played by men and women in all aspects of SALW control.
- Account for gendered security perceptions, attitudes, and behaviors towards small arms and light weapons.
- Tailor strategies to target different groups based on their knowledge, attitudes, and behaviors regarding small arms and light weapons and their influence on other groups.
- Recognize and support local initiatives, including peacebuilding and violence prevention activities by grassroots citizens' organizations, many led by women and youth.

The Role of Women's Groups

Women's civil society organizations should play a central role in small arms and light weapons control initiatives. They can provide gender-relevant insights into policies and projects, facilitating the integration of a gender perspective. They can also address social problems resulting from minor arms misuse, such as offering counseling for victims of minor arms violence or creating grassroots community initiatives to protect children in areas plagued by gang violence. Women's groups should participate in long-term efforts to build peace education, non-violent conflict resolution capacities, and tolerance. They should also engage in short-term efforts to raise awareness about the dangers associated with the possession and use of small arms. Additionally, they should be involved in the oversight, monitoring, and evaluation of small arms and light weapons control efforts.

The Role of Men's Groups

When designing peace education programs and building capacity for armed violence prevention, it is crucial to recognize the close connection between small arms and traditional perceptions of masculinity, identity, and culture. Understanding men's motivation for owning, using, and misusing small arms. Men have a critical role in engaging other men, especially marginalized young men and those at risk of marginalization, in constructive dialogues. These dialogues should address how socialized masculinity can have detrimental effects on men themselves, the women in their lives, and the overall development potential of communities, societies, and countries. Initiatives led by men that oppose violence against women, promote gender equality, empower women, and endorse positive, non-violent expressions of masculinity should be supported and integrated into existing small arms and light weapons control efforts.

The Role of the Media

Small arms are often depicted in various forms of media aimed at young men, including television, films, video games, and music videos. Emerging evidence suggests a connection between media violence and real-world violence. Young men are the primary consumers of violent media, often portraying small arms as instruments of violence. Consequently:

- The media's role in perpetuating gender stereotypes and influencing attitudes toward small arms should be recognized.
- Sensitize journalists to the gender-specific impacts of minor arms possession and misuse.
- Raise awareness among journalists on topics such as human rights, women's rights, global norms, and international instruments related

to gender, armed violence, small arms, and light weapons control.

- Promote media support for small arms and light weapons control efforts, especially those addressing gender-specific impacts.
- Regulate the broadcasting of violence on television and its depiction in film, video games, and other media, including violence against women and sexual violence.
- Promote programs that encourage tolerance, non-violent expressions of masculinity, gender equality, and non-violent conflict resolution.

Survivor Assistance

Survivors are individuals who have experienced physical injuries, intimidation, or brutality due to violence involving small arms or light weapons. Survivor assistance encompasses emergency and ongoing medical care, physical rehabilitation, psychological and social support, access to justice, and economic reintegration.

Caring for Survivors

Caring for survivors typically falls on women and girls as mothers, wives, sisters, daughters, and partners. This caregiving role can limit their educational and economic opportunities and impact their health. Family members, particularly women and girls, may become frontline caregivers, leading to additional pressure, especially in settings with limited or costly services. Household stress may exacerbate poverty, and the unequal earning power between men and women can worsen the situation.

Female-Headed Households

Gun violence often results in more female-headed households due to the disproportionate number of men killed or impaired and unable to work, which can negatively affect the education of children and young people, leading to school dropouts or involvement in risky behaviors to contribute to household income. Male unemployment can also exacerbate violence against women.

Psycho-social Support

Injuries and disabilities from minor arms violence are associated with psychological issues. However, psycho-social interventions or mental health programs may face challenges due to social customs, perceptions of gender roles, and the stigma experienced by survivors.

Economic Reintegration

Priority should be given to male and female survivors of minor arms violence in livelihood programs such as vocational training and employment, especially those related to survivor assistance and small arms and light weapons control. Survivor assistance should include public awareness and education to prevent and combat discrimination against survivors, particularly as they attempt to reintegrate into the workforce.

Survivors as Agents of Change

Male and female survivors can be powerful agents of change in addressing small arms and light weapons misuse. Those willing to do so should receive support advocating for effective small arms and light weapons control. Survivor associations should be supported to strengthen their capacity for service delivery, advocacy, and management.

Review Questions

1. What are the primary categories of voluntary weapons collection programs, and provide examples of their implementation?
2. How do international organizations, governments, and civil society groups collaborate to ensure the success of weapons collection programs?
3. What are the gender-related consequences of cross-border conflicts in Africa, and how have small arms exacerbated gender-based violence?
4. How have small arms disrupted traditional gender roles in conflict zones, and why are lightweight firearms particularly significant in this context?
5. What is known about gender differences in attitudes toward the widespread presence of small arms, and why is it important to study

these attitudes?

6. What practical strategies are needed to address the impact of small arms and light weapons on gender-specific violence and social norms?

Discussion Points

1. Explore the ethical and practical implications of offering incentives in weapons collection programs, such as cash exchanges or amnesty. How do these incentives impact the effectiveness of such programs?

2. Discuss the role of gender stereotypes in influencing attitudes toward firearms and their impact on women's and men's roles in conflict zones.

3. How can the media play a role in either perpetuating or challenging gender norms related to small arms ownership and use? What steps can be taken to sensitize journalists and promote gender-sensitive media coverage?

4. Consider the challenges and opportunities for survivor assistance in the context of minor arms violence. How can gender-sensitive approaches be integrated into support programs for survivors?

CHAPTER FIVE: GENDER-RESPONSIVE STRATEGIES FOR SALW GOVERNANCE

Summary of Chapter Five

1. Government's Role in SALW Control: Governments play a central role in controlling Small Arms and Light Weapons (SALW). They should promote gender equality, involve women and men in decision-making, establish coordinating bodies, and address gender aspects in SALW control strategies.

2. Civil Society's Contribution: Civil society organizations, especially those focused on gender, are essential in promoting local ownership, offering insights, and garnering support for SALW control. Women's organizations, in particular, can raise awareness, influence policies, and participate in disarmament and peace-building programs.

3. Regional Organizations and Coordination: Regional organizations are crucial in addressing the cross-border nature of SALW issues. They should base their policies on gender-sensitive assessments, promote data collection disaggregated by sex, and ensure women's participation at all levels.

4. UN's Involvement: UN organizations should integrate gender considerations into SALW control projects and programs. They must advocate for gender-specific data collection, support civil society organizations, allocate resources for gender training, and coordinate efforts through

the UN Coordinating Action on Small Arms (CASA) mechanism.

5. Donors' Role: Donors are essential in supporting national SALW control efforts, especially in low-income and post-conflict settings. They should encourage governments to fulfill international agreements related to gender issues, provide capacity-building support, and ensure their initiatives incorporate gender perspectives.

6. UNDP's Eight-Point Agenda for Gender Equality: The UNDP has an eight-point agenda for gender equality in crisis prevention. It covers various aspects like ending violence against women, advancing gender justice, expanding women's participation and leadership, building peace with and for women, promoting gender equality in disaster risk reduction, ensuring gender-responsive recovery, transforming government, and developing capacities for social change.

Gender Roles of Key SALW Control Stakeholders

Government

The primary responsibility for controlling SALW rests with the respective states. It's crucial for governments to promote gender equality and women's empowerment across all governmental departments, including involving women and men in decision-making roles in activities related to gender awareness, education, advocacy, and capacity building. To effectively manage small arms control, governments should establish a national coordinating body, as outlined in MOSAIC 03.40, "National Coordinating Mechanisms on Small Arms and Light Weapons." This coordinating body should:

- Include government departments responsible for women's affairs, health, education, and social policy.
- Incorporate civil society organizations focusing on gender and women's

issues.

- Analyze and address small arms and light weapons control from a gender perspective, especially issues related to demand.
- Ensure that national strategies and action plans for small arms and light weapons control align with the gender-specific guidance provided by MOSAIC 04.10, "Designing and Implementing National Action Plans."
- Guarantee the equal and full participation of women in decision-making processes related to small arms and light weapons control, potentially co-opting competent female experts from civil society groups.
- Initiate capacity-building activities to enhance women's knowledge of small arms and light weapons control.
- Create an environment where both men and women can freely express their views on small arms and light weapons control, including through public dialogues, consultations, polls, and surveys.
- Provide financial and technical assistance to civil society groups, particularly those working on gender and women's issues, strengthening their capacity to undertake advocacy, violence prevention, peace-building, education, tolerance, and victim assistance programs supporting small arms and light weapons control.
- Address the vulnerabilities of young men to engaging in and being victimized by armed violence, supporting educational, employment, sporting, and artistic opportunities for low-income young men, and promoting non-violent models of masculinity.
- Hold law enforcement officials accountable for the safe, secure, and appropriate use of state-owned weapons, especially when off duty, and ensure compliance with the United Nations Basic Principles on the Use of Force and Firearms by Law Enforcement Officials.
- Train police on their roles and responsibilities under relevant national laws regarding the presence and use of small arms in the context of intimate partner and domestic/family-related violence, including informing victims of their rights.
- Incorporate a gender perspective into issuing and renewing small arms licenses to civilians, in line with MOSAIC 03.30, "National Regulation of

Civilian Access to Small Arms and Light Weapons."

- Raise public awareness about the risks associated with the possession, proliferation, and misuse of small arms and light weapons, particularly concerning campaigns to prevent intimate partner and domestic/family-related violence and promote a culture of peace, as detailed in MOSAIC 04.30, "Awareness-Raising."
- Include gender aspects of small arms and light weapons control when reporting on the implementation of the United Nations Programme of Action to Prevent, Combat, and Eradicate the Illicit Trade in Small Arms and Light Weapons in All Its Aspects, as per MOSAIC 04.40, "Monitoring, Evaluation, and Reporting."
- Allocate sufficient budget resources for implementing the above initiatives, integrating gender-responsive budgeting into all policy stages.

Civil Society

Civil society plays a crucial role in SALW control, promoting local ownership, offering valuable insights, and garnering support for control efforts. Civil society organizations specializing in gender can enhance gender-responsive small arms and light weapons control efforts by:

- Lobbying for and providing gender-responsive advice in policy development.
- Monitoring the implementation of international, regional, national, and local policies related to gender mainstreaming and gender equality in the context of small arms and light weapons control.
- Promoting women's political participation, decision-making, and leadership in small arms and light weapons policy.
- Providing capacity-building on gender and security issues, facilitating dialogue and negotiation between local communities and government institutions, and raising public awareness of small arms and light weapons

control processes and activities.

- Collaborating with survivors, perpetrators, and affected communities to address the demand for small arms and light weapons and the detrimental impact of their misuse.
- Conducting gender-sensitive surveys and assessments on issues related to small arms and light weapons.
- Ensuring that the specific concerns of men and women are voiced at local, national, and international levels.
- Actively participating in small arms and light weapons surveys and weapons collection and destruction processes, contributing to trust and confidence-building among men and women.

Women's organizations, in particular, can contribute by:

- Raising awareness of the risks associated with the possession, proliferation, and misuse of small arms and light weapons, contributing to public debate, and advocating for changes in a country's policies related to these weapons.
- Influencing their homes and communities by encouraging their children, partners, and family members to turn in illicit and unwanted small arms and light weapons.
- Initiating and participating in community forums on small arms control, ensuring that local leaders, representatives of international organizations, and others hear women's perspectives.
- Lobbying national governments to sign international treaties related to small arms and light weapons and implement their commitments under those treaties.
- Designing innovative programs and projects that provide community incentives for former combatants, including female fighters, to disarm, demobilize, and reintegrate into their communities.
- Encouraging ex-combatants to lay down arms and participate in weapons collection programs, ensuring they benefit from any incentives provided for such activities.

- Ensuring that women's participation and expertise actively inform decisions related to small arms control processes, transitional justice strategies, and forming legislative and decision-making forums.
- Involve women in the design, implementation, monitoring, and evaluation of initiatives to control small arms and light weapons.

Regional Organizations

As SALW can easily cross borders, regional approaches, including the coordination and harmonization of laws and practices, are crucial for adequate control. Regional organizations play a significant role in building consensus, advancing regional and global norms on small arms and light weapons control, and mobilizing resources for states to address this issue. When developing and implementing regional approaches, regional organizations should:

- Base their policy development on a gender-sensitive assessment of the impact of small arms and light weapons on men, women, boys, and girls.
- Promote systematic data collection that disaggregates information by sex and age to understand the direct and indirect impacts of the misuse of these weapons.
- Ensure women's participation in policy development, decision-making, planning, implementation, monitoring, and evaluation processes.
- Foster connections and knowledge-sharing among relevant civil society groups, especially those working on gender and women's issues, to enhance regional networks.

Regional organizations may also:

- Support the establishment of regional observatories on small arms and light weapons proliferation and misuse, encouraging their collaboration with other regional observatories and those focusing on gender and women's issues.
- Provide technical assistance and financial resources to enhance states'

capacities in addressing gender aspects of small arms and light weapons control within the region.

The United Nations

All United Nations organizations, including Funds, Programs, and Specialized Agencies, are mandated to support gender equality. UN organizations involved in small arms and light weapons control should integrate gender considerations at all stages of their projects and programs. They should also:

- Highlight the impact of uncontrolled small arms and light weapons proliferation and misuse on other programmatic areas covered by the United Nations.
- Promote the integration of gender-specific considerations into UN programming related to small arms and light weapons control.
- Advocate for systematic data collection that disaggregates information by sex and age to conduct gender analyses of the problem.
- Mainstream gender at the operational level when designing small arms and light weapons projects and assist national coordinating mechanisms in mainstreaming gender into their National Action Plans for control.
- Support the participation of civil society organizations, particularly those addressing gender, youth, and women's issues, at global, regional, national, and local levels in small arms and light weapons control efforts.
- Allocate adequate resources for training on gender issues to build the capacity of their staff regarding gender aspects of small arms and light weapons control.
- Ensure a coherent and coordinated approach to their work on small arms and light weapons control through the UN Coordinating Action on Small Arms (CASA) mechanism.
- Share and disseminate sex- and age-disaggregated data related to small arms and light weapons across the UN system and with partners at various levels.
- Include qualitative and quantitative information on gender aspects of

small arms and light weapons control in relevant reports and recommendations on policy and operational issues.

- Provide technical assistance to states to enhance their capacity to integrate a gender perspective into their legislative and policy frameworks related to small arms and light weapons control.

Donors

Donors are crucial in supporting national small arms and light weapons control efforts, especially in low-income and post-conflict countries. In collaboration with international organizations and civil society, donors should:

- Encourage governments to ratify international agreements related to women's human rights or assist them in fulfilling their obligations under such agreements, which include various conventions and resolutions.
- Ensure that the small arms and light weapons control initiatives they support fully incorporate gender issues and encourage women's active participation.
- Equip relevant staff in international development and foreign affairs ministries with gender expertise.
- Support further research on gender and small arms and light weapons control.
- Donors may also provide capacity-building support, either as part of comprehensive security sector reform or in response to a small arms and light weapons control gender assessment, which may involve:
- Training law enforcement officials, including addressing gender issues related to minor arms misuse.
- Developing judicial systems to enhance their capacity to address gender-based violence and related issues.

UNDP Eight-Point Agenda for Gender Equality in Crisis Prevention

A.1 Strengthening Women's Security in Crisis: Ending Violence Against Women

- Violence against women violates human rights, decency, and dignity.
- Rape and sexual violence are not unintended consequences; they are deliberate tactics of warfare. Perpetrators of these crimes must be held accountable by communities, governments, and the international community.
- Violence against women hinders progress in poverty eradication, HIV/AIDS prevention, and peace and security.
- Men and boys have a crucial role in combating the violence pandemic against women.

A.2 Advancing Gender Justice: Ensuring Justice and Security for Women

- Laws protecting women's rights should be part of and enforced within legal frameworks.
- Women should know their rights and access to legal systems, possibly through free legal services.
- Cultural, traditional, or religious beliefs should never excuse or justify violence against women.

A.3 Expanding Women's Citizenship, Participation, and Leadership: Empowering Women as Decision-Makers.

- Women need skills and confidence to influence decisions affecting their lives, including direct participation in government and the security sector.
- Women often face barriers in accessing business opportunities and land ownership negotiations. Legislation must change to support women's business and land ownership.
- Women's representation in social, political, and economic spheres is

essential for their voices in peace and recovery processes.

A.4 Building Peace with and for Women: Involving Women in All Peace Processes

- Women must participate in all stages of peace and recovery processes, including high-level negotiations.
- Peace agreements offer opportunities for inclusiveness, democratic reform, and gender equality, which should be prioritized.
- Peace agreements should include gender provisions and prioritize their implementation.
- A.5 Promoting Gender Equality in Disaster Risk Reduction: Supporting Women and Men to Rebuild Better
- Disaster risk analysis should consider women's unique needs.
- Steps should be taken to prevent the increased vulnerability of women and girls as community structures weaken and violence escalates.
- Recovery efforts should consider women's economic potential, for example, by targeting women-headed households in cash-for-work schemes.
- Temporary housing should respect women's privacy to avoid exploitation and discrimination, which affect the well-being of women and children.
- Women's experience and knowledge should be valued and integrated into plans and policies.

A.6 Ensuring Gender-Responsive Recovery: Empowering Women as Recovery Leaders

- Women should have equal access to livelihoods, including land and credit opportunities. Rebuilding key sectors should specifically benefit women.

A.7 Transforming Government to Deliver for Women: Including Women's Issues in the National Agenda

- Women should be engaged in decision-making regarding government budgets and resource mobilization.

- Incentives should be provided to public institutions addressing women's needs.

A.8 Developing Capacities for Social Change: Collaborating to Transform Society

- Women's organizations and networks should be strengthened for responsiveness and accountability on gender issues.
- Men should be educated to promote gender equality and support women's empowerment.

To achieve this Eight-Point Agenda:

- Support full implementation of Security Council Resolution 1325.
- Incorporate gender equality priorities into advocacy and strategic planning in development, humanitarian, peace, and security.
- Strengthen human resources, policies, and programs for responsiveness and accountability on gender issues.
- Build partnerships to maximize impact on gender priorities.
- Develop gender-responsive funding mechanisms and resource mobilization strategies.
- Support data collection that focuses on women's perspectives and values.
- Advanced intellectual leadership, knowledge management, and monitoring and evaluation of gender and crisis prevention and recovery (CPR) issues.

Gender-Responsive SALW Program Indicators

Comprehensive, gender-responsive monitoring and evaluation of small arms and light weapons control and armed violence reduction programs are essential to assess the impact of policies and interventions on men, women, boys, and girls, identify lessons learned, and address unforeseen positive and negative effects.

Gender-Responsive Interventions - Key considerations for ensuring that small arms and light weapons control interventions are gender-responsive include:

- Addressing the specific needs of women, girls, marginalized men, and boys.
- Promoting increased participation of women in planned interventions.
- Monitoring gender-related objectives and the impact of gender activities through specific indicators.
- Allocating funds for gender objectives, activities, and outputs.
- Involving gender expertise in intervention design.
- Adding women's NGOs in SALW control programs as collaborators.
- Identifying and addressing interventions to reduce minor arms violence in homes and prevent armed gender-based violence.

Gender-Responsive Monitoring and Evaluation Process

Gender Mainstreaming - Key questions for ensuring that the monitoring and evaluation process of small arms and light weapons control interventions are gender-responsive include:

- Assessing the capacity of monitoring and evaluation staff to integrate gender issues.
- Ensuring sex and age data disaggregation in monitoring and evaluation, addressing specific gender aspects such as gender roles and gender-based violence.

- Evaluating the achievement of gender-related objectives, indicators, and benchmarks.
- Training field research teams to collect information from men and women.
- Analyzing the overall impact of interventions on men, women, boys, and girls.
- Identifying good and bad practices related to gender issues for future programming.
- Communicating evaluation results to participants and affected communities, with mechanisms for collecting feedback.

Promoting Equal Participation of Women and Men

- Ensuring equal participation of men and women in monitoring and evaluation.
- Implementing measures to reach marginalized groups in monitoring and evaluation.
- Assessing the extent to which men and women were involved in the program and if their views were incorporated.
- Examining the program's impact on men and women's participation in small arms and light weapons control processes.

Gender Aspects of Results and Process

Key indicators to measure gender aspects of intervention results and processes may include:

Public Health Impacts

- Disaggregated death and injury rates related to firearms by sex and age (homicide, suicide, unintended shootings).

- Psychosocial and psychological trauma related to armed violence disaggregated by sex and age.
- Security Needs, Perceptions, and Priorities of Men, Women, Girls, and Boys
- Relative perceptions of security and danger.
- Levels of fear related to specific armed actors/groups.
- Confidence in the security sector's ability.
- Perceived need for small arms ownership for self-protection.
- Perceptions of arms availability in the community.
- Actual numbers of small arms in the community/country and typology of small arms owners.
- Involvement of women and girls in small arms and light weapons smuggling.
- Attitudes towards small arms and light weapons possession, exhibition, and use.
- Social customs valuing small arms use violence and violent masculinity.
- Typology of gang members, including women, boys, and girls.
- Media representation of men, women, boys, and girls in small arms and light weapons issues.

- Violence Against Boys and Girls
- Rates of direct violence-related death and injury among boys and girls.
- Rates of unintentional firearm death and injury among boys and girls.
- Incidence of psychosocial and psychological trauma associated with minor arms violence disaggregated by gender.
- Presence of boys and girls in fighting forces, armed groups, and gangs, including their functions.
- Incidence of armed forced recruitment of boys and girls.
- Many men, women, boys, and girls are victims of trafficking networks involved in small arms and light weapons smuggling.

Violence Against and Among Men and Women

- Prevalence of use of firearms in violence against and among men and women.
- Rates of young men and women injured or killed through minor arms violence.
- Incidents and typology of violence in the home, including those involving firearms.
- Small arms-related intentional and unintentional death and injury rates disaggregated by gender.
- Psychosocial and psychological trauma associated with armed violence, including threats and small arms 'brandishing,' by gender and age.
- Rates of successfully prosecuted gender-based violence cases.
- Existence of gender-based violence prevention measures.
- The number of men, women, boys, and girls victims of trafficking networks involved in small arms and light weapons smuggling.

Impacts on Humanitarian and Development Assistance

- Percentage of the population out of reach of humanitarian aid agencies, disaggregated by gender.
- Small arms-related mortality and injuries among aid workers.
- Incidents of armed robberies, rapes, or other crimes.
- Psychological trauma linked to minor arms violence.
- Perceptions of security.
- Perceptions of arms availability in the community.
- The actual number of small arms in the community.

Refugees and Internally Displaced People

- Incidence of firearm related death, injury, and disability among displaced people, disaggregated by sex.

- Armed intimidation (may require case definition) and assault among displaced people.
- Armed sexual violence against women and men reported or observed.
- Dependence of displaced populations on food aid due to an insecure situation.
- Existence of female-specific health services and facilities in camps and their capacity to respond to armed violence injuries and trauma.

Governance

- Women's role and participation in community and local organizations and structures.
- Women's participation in national decision-making structures, by level.
- Implementation of international agreements on women's rights.
- Attention is given to mainstreaming gender in new legislation.
- Women's and gender-based civil society participation in advocacy and public awareness.
- Capacity gaps in civil society and especially women's organizations to fully and effectively participate in small arms and light weapons control.
- Ratio of female staff in security institutions and the military.

Social

- Boys' and girls' enrollment rates in primary and secondary education.
- Changes in the quality and accessibility of social services and their gendered implications.
- Women's and men's belief in fair treatment from institutions.
- The gender-responsiveness of existing security and justice laws, policies, and institutions and improvements in gender-responsiveness (considering progress made).

- Changes in the gender division of labor within households.
- Changes in social attitudes toward women in leadership positions.
- The influence of women and men in community decision-making.
- The number and typology of women employed in small arms and light weapons manufacturing.

UNDP Gender-Mainstreaming Checklist for Policy and Project Documents

Background and Justification

Is the document's background information highlighting the gender dimension of the intervention?

Does the justification provide compelling arguments for gender mainstreaming and promoting gender equality?

Goals

- Does the intervention's goal address the needs of both men and women?
- Does the goal aim to rectify gender imbalances by addressing the practical needs of both genders?
- Does the goal seek to transform institutions, including social ones, perpetuating gender inequality?

Target Beneficiaries

Unless specific gender corrective measures exist, is there a gender balance among the target beneficiaries?

Objectives

Do the intervention objectives cater to the needs of both women and men?

Activities

- Do the planned activities involve both women and men?
- Are additional activities required to ensure that a gender perspective is explicit (e.g., gender training, additional research)?

Indicators

- Are indicators in place to measure progress toward each objective?
- Do these indicators encompass the gender aspects of each objective?
- Are the indicators gender disaggregated?
- Are targets set to ensure adequate gender balance in activities (e.g., quotas for male and female participation)?

Implementation

- Who will implement the planned intervention?
- Have these partners undergone gender-mainstreaming training to sustain a gender perspective during implementation?
- Will both women and men participate in the implementation?

Monitoring and Evaluation

- Does the monitoring and evaluation strategy incorporate a gender perspective?
- Will it assess both substantive (content) and administrative (process) aspects of the intervention?

Risks

- Have potential risks related to gender roles and relations within society been considered (e.g., stereotypes or structural barriers hindering full gender participation)?
- Has the potential negative impact of the intervention been assessed (e.g., potential increased burden on women or social isolation of men)?

Budget

- Have financial inputs been reviewed to ensure that both men and women benefit from the planned intervention?
- Include gender sensitivity training or engagement of short-term gender experts in budget allocations.

Annexes

Are any relevant research papers or excerpts included as annexes, especially those justifying the focus on gender?

Communication Strategy

Has a communication strategy been developed to inform various stake-holders about the project's existence, progress, and results from a gender perspective?

Review Questions

1. What is the primary responsibility of governments in controlling SALW, and how can they promote gender equality in this context?
2. How do civil society organizations, especially those focused on gender, contribute to SALW control efforts?
3. Why is regional coordination essential in addressing SALW issues, and what role do regional organizations play?
4. What specific actions should UN organizations take to integrate gender considerations into SALW control projects and programs?
5. How can donors support national SALW control efforts, and what role should gender play in their initiatives?
6. Explain the UNDP's Eight-Point Agenda for Gender Equality in Crisis Prevention and its significance in the context of SALW control.

Discussion Points

1. Discuss the challenges and opportunities in implementing gender-responsive strategies for SALW governance at the national level.
2. Explore the role of women's organizations in advocating for disarmament, peace-building, and policy changes related to SALW control.
3. Analyze the importance of regional coordination in addressing the transnational aspects of SALW proliferation and misuse.
4. Discuss the potential impact of gender-responsive initiatives by donors and the UN in enhancing SALW control efforts, particularly in post-conflict regions.

CHAPTER SIX: GENDER-BASED VIOLENCE IN POST-CONFLICT REGIONS

Summary of Chapter Six

1. Gender-Based Violence in Post-Conflict Regions: Sexual and gender-based violence is prevalent in post-conflict regions, with historical acceptance of violence against women as a societal norm. Understanding gender is crucial, encompassing issues of violence beyond just equality. Gender roles and customs play a significant role in violence.

2. Empowerment Approach: Women's empowerment is central to development, focusing on "power within" rather than "power over." Both men and women should be involved in empowering efforts to challenge existing power structures.

3. The Ubiquity of Violence: Violence knows no boundaries, affecting people regardless of social class, race, or age. Domestic violence and sexual and gender-based violence are pervasive issues affecting women and men. Different cultures may accommodate various forms of violence.

4. Civil Society Response: Civil society, particularly NGOs, is critical in addressing gender-based violence in post-conflict regions. The bottom-up approach to women's empowerment is essential to fill the gaps left by government efforts.

5. Reproductive Health and Society: Post-conflict regions often struggle with addressing women's reproductive health and violence issues

resulting from war-related challenges and social norms. Inadequate reproductive health education, limited access to contraceptives, and other issues persist.

6. Case of Bosnia and Herzegovina: Family violence is an ongoing problem in Bosnia and Herzegovina, with various studies revealing the extent of domestic violence. SOS telephone services and NGOs play a crucial role in providing support to victims.

Sexual and Gender-Based Violence in Post-Conflict Regions

Sexual and gender-based violence (SGBV) is a harsh reality in post-conflict regions worldwide. Post-conflict regions have grappled with the challenge of addressing violence both publicly and institutionally. Historically, women endured violence as an integral part of social and moral norms, and society accepted this status quo, as did men. For instance, violence within marriage is an accepted practice and a morally unquestionable right in some cultures. This cycle of domestic violence, often passed from father to son, persisted across generations.

Understanding Gender

Gender issues are intricate and extend beyond mere equality and equity for women. In the context of the United Nations, gender perspectives and practical standpoints are examined while addressing various forms of violence, including sexual abuse, physical and psychological violence, organizational violence, and others. It is essential to consider the impact of regional customs and practices on violence issues. Analyzing violence through a gender-specific lens involves more than comprehending the consequences and implications of gender role expectations and stereotypes.

Empowerment Approach– Power-within Vs Power-over: Many United

Nations conferences have advocated making women's empowerment central to development processes. For example, the International Conference on Population and Development (ICPD) in Cairo discussed the population issue not merely as a technical demographic problem but as a choice tied to women's empowerment regarding their health and reproductive rights. However, empowering women should not exclude men from the process. Gender equality discourse promotes the involvement of both men and women in organizations and movements. In mainstream development discourse, empowerment focuses on entrepreneurship, self-reliance, and challenging power structures that subordinate women are often overlooked. However, empowerment has to involve transforming power structures, and women must develop "power within," which includes building self-esteem, raising awareness, and boosting confidence. This approach contrasts with "power over," which signifies confrontations between the powerful (primarily men) and the powerless (mainly women).

Gender in Context: This emphasizes empowerment as a bottom-up process rather than a top-down strategy. It becomes a tool for women to empower themselves. Developmental agencies should facilitate women's implementation of their empowerment by providing clear policies, programs, and incentives. Viewing gender as a means to empower women's reproductive health can help reduce gender and sexual-based violence. Although obstacles exist, changing policy frameworks, organizational structures, and processes can pave the way for women's empowerment.

The Ubiquity of Violence

Violence is a global phenomenon that knows no boundaries, affecting individu als regardless of their social class, race, ethnicity, locality, or age. Throughout history, men and women have experienced abuse, exploitation, harassment, torture, and even death, mainly in the context of Domestic Violence (DV) and Sexual and Gender-Based Violence (SGBV). Women face violence in various settings, from thatched huts to skyscraper apartments, while men suffer violence in concentration camps and prisons. Rape does not discriminate and occurs in a range of places. These stark realities include women being raped in college dorms, back alleys, and bedrooms. People, including children, have been sold into slavery and subjected to various forms of sexual exploitation. The perspective on violence differs between genders. Women's experiences often revolve around issues of control, encompassing emotional, sexual, and physical abuse with explicit and implicit dimensions. In contrast, men typically view violence as isolated, primarily physical incidents.

Violence against women/girls is a widespread global problem. Between 20 percent and 60 percent of women report experiencing partner violence, with underreporting being expected due to various factors. GBV encompasses physical, sexual, and emotional abuse of women, sexual abuse of female children, marital rape, sexual assault, forced prostitution, and trafficking of women and young girls. Forms of violence vary from culture to culture and are primarily accommodated in most cultures. The reality is that women spend most of their lives recovering from, resisting, or surviving violence rather than creating and thriving. A perspective suggests that violence against women/girls starts with sex-selective abortion and infanticide in countries where girls are valued less than boys or considered an economic burden. Notably, these statements focus on violence prevention for women despite men being victims of violence as well. Sexual violence is used continually in concentration camps and prisons against both male and female inmates as a method of control.

Civil Society and Its Response to Violence

The bottom-up approach to women's empowerment "within" necessitates robust engagement from non-governmental organizations (NGOs) operating in post-conflict regions. This approach arises from the frustration of integrating gender into mainstream development policies and programs globally. In conflict zones, gender issues are often misunderstood in a cultural context and introduced into humanitarian aid and development programs as predetermined "packages." Post-conflict regions have the advantage of nurturing civil society and cultivating innovative ideas and capacities, in contrast to government efforts hampered by war. In Bosnia and Herzegovina, after the war nearly obliterated infrastructure, humanitarian aid was administered through volunteer groups that quickly aligned with various NGOs. Many NGOs in Bosnia and Herzegovina focus on issues related to violence, with over 14 NGOs dedicated to women's issues and gender-based educational activities. These humanitarian agencies play a significant role in addressing violence against women. Nevertheless, domestic violence persists.

While gender equality remains an elusive goal in the Balkans, the post-war period prompted a reassessment of this issue, placing it high on the social agenda. However, implementing the gender perspective is still in its infancy. This concept goes beyond addressing women's discrimination and rights violations, recognizing that men were also victims of abuse during the war. The torture endured in concentration camps affected both men and women significantly. In the Sarajevo Canton, of the 6,000 concentration camp victims, 5,000 were men, with an alarming 80 percent of them reportedly experiencing rape. Extensive literature and research confirm the mistreatment of women during and after the war. Unfortunately, little attention has been given to men who, like women, are victims of sexual violence.

Another aspect of women in post-conflict societies is their persistently disadvantaged position, rooted in patriarchy, which assigns different roles and behaviors to women and men. Gender identities, denoting roles and behavior allocated to women and men serve as tools for distributing power within society and the family. Thus, gender identities are largely culturally created and subject to shifts, changes, and adjustments.

A common assumption, based on feminist thought, suggests that men are inherently aggressive and violent while women are passive and peaceful. However, this perception of women as inherently against war has been challenged. Conflicts in the Balkan region have shown that several women supported the war but did so differently from their partners directly involved in the conflict. In 1991, the image of Serbian women cheering on their husbands, sons, brothers, and fathers heading to fight in Croatia remained a potent and enduring memory of the war. Conversely, Serbian women who protested the war at Belgrade's central square represent another vivid image.

The notion that men are exclusively pro-conflict is also challenged historically, as male soldiers often had the most to lose in conflicts. Those who failed to meet societal expectations of bravery faced stigma and severe punishment from both men and women. During conflicts in the Balkan region, many men, particularly young men, fled their countries to avoid fighting. These men continue to face harsh consequences for contributing to the conflict. In Serbia, defectors are labeled ethnic traitors, the most severe stigma in Serbian culture. In Bosnia and Herzegovina, defectors are frequently blocked, making it challenging to secure employment and subjecting them to verbal abuse. Women's reluctance to participate in conflict and violence can be attributed to their exclusion from political and social life, decision-making processes, and economic dependence on men. Women remain primarily responsible for family care and social assistance duties. As a result, women took the lead in assisting in the conflict, marking the emergence of civil societies in the Balkans.

Reproductive Health and Society

Both violence and women's reproductive health issues are often inadequately addressed in post-conflict societies, both at the societal and family levels. With the international community's focus on the Balkans, there is a growing acknowledgment of the need to address violence and reproductive health for the benefit of the population. Post-conflict regions face challenges such as impoverishment, significantly when productive infrastructure has been damaged. During the conflict, women and children experienced numerous hardships that persisted in the post-conflict setting. Inadequate reproductive health education, limited access to contraceptives, taboo attitudes toward human sexuality, low-quality reproductive health services, unequal distribution of services, the lack of modern diagnostic facilities, and widespread non-medical abortions (due to a lack of birth control methods) are common problems with severe repercussions for women's health. HIV/AIDS and other sexually transmitted diseases are seldom monitored or recorded, and health services struggle to maintain pre-war standards.

The Case of Bosnia and Herzegovina

Domestic Violence in Bosnia and Herzegovina

Family violence is not a new or rare occurrence in Bosnian and Herzegovinian society. Violence against women did not originate with the war but is an ongoing issue hidden from public awareness and thus left unaddressed. It is a neglected problem in many societies. Several studies on family violence in Sarajevo indicate male involvement, but these findings are not thoroughly analyzed. In 2000, the Women to Women NGO surveyed violence against women in Sarajevo. 24 percent of the 160 respondents were men because most men approached for participation reportedly declined. In the survey, one question addressed gender differences in attitudes toward reducing the number of perpetrators of violence against women. Approximately 15 percent of respondents emphasized the importance of educating perpetrators of violence, but the analysis did not specify how many of these respondents were men. All other questions exclusively focused on women's needs and perceptions of solutions to the problem.

Numerous studies conducted during the post-war period have addressed the effects of violence after the war. Medica Zenica, a leading NGO in the field, conducted an extensive study on violence against women, with a broad definition encompassing domestic violence, sexual assault, trafficking, and sexual harassment. The study revealed the pervasive nature of violence in society and its interconnectedness, which stems from the societal structure, echoing similar trends worldwide. While Medica's research predominantly focused on domestic violence, sexual assault, sexual harassment, incest, and prostitution, it excluded other forms of violence, such as power imbalances and human trafficking. Nonetheless, these issues are investigated by NGOs through SOS telephone services in several major cities in Bosnia and Herzegovina.

Medica Zenica was among the first NGOs to conceptualize and address domestic violence in the region. They conducted in-depth interviews with 542 women in Zenica municipality to assess how violence against women had impacted their lives. The research encompassed demographic profiles, socioeconomic status, violence prevalence, community service evaluation, and women's reflections on violence. While the study's sample only represented one town, Zenica, and the findings may not be generalizable to the entire country, they underscore the need for further research. The study also highlighted the lack of appropriate services available to victims, stressing the importance of raising public awareness about women's rights to live free from violence, especially within the private sphere. Additionally, developing contemporary reproductive health services by enhancing existing services and educating professionals and policymakers, particularly politicians, was deemed crucial.

Another NGO, Women of Bosnia and Herzegovina, conducted similar research on violence against women in Mostar. Of the 1,000 women interviewed, nearly half (48.8 percent) had experienced violence either directly or indirectly. Family violence remains a significant issue in the region, with post-war challenges exacerbating the situation. These challenges include family breakdowns, difficulties reintegrating into post-war families, alcoholism, war trauma, educational gaps, post-conflict economic hardship, and moral despair. The consequences of family violence are devastating, taking a toll on victims' physical and mental health.

The research from Medica reflected that domestic violence, excluding child abuse, is highly prevalent; one in five women (23 percent) in the sample had been physically abused by her partner, with nearly one in four (24 percent) experiencing prolonged battering. While the sample was representative of only one town, Zenica, and may not be generalized to the entire country, it underscores the pressing need for further research. These extensive studies on violence against women reveal deeply rooted problems in post-conflict societies. Additionally, the role of NGOs and civil society in addressing these issues is instrumental, as they fill gaps left by government efforts and facilitate the necessary changes for progress.

Services and Assistance Through SOS Telephones

After the war, the first organized effort to address domestic violence in Bosnia and Herzegovina emerged in the form of SOS telephone services. In 1997, the International Rescue Committee (IRC) collaborated with the women's NGO Anima to launch the SOS phone service in the town of Gorazde in central Bosnia. This service was designed to support women facing violence, offering a listening ear, advice, counseling, encouragement, and referrals for further assistance. Subsequently, SOS services expanded across the country, and today, there are eight SOS centers located in various communities in Bosnia and Herzegovina, including Banja Luka, Mostar, Zenica, Gorazde, Tuzla, and Sarajevo. Notably, two of these centers in Sarajevo also provide SOS telephone services tailored to assist children. Initially, the SOS telephone service in Mostar addressed a wide range of inquiries. However, in 1999, it transitioned to focus exclusively on issues related to violence against women.

Impact and Role of SOS Services

In 2001, the NGO Women for Women analyzed 81 SOS client calls, revealing that a majority of the callers had experienced domestic violence. It was found that one-third of these women were economically dependent on their spouses, and 18 of them secured jobs after receiving assistance from SOS professionals. SOS telephone services in Zenica and Sarajevo have incorporated counseling components into their programs, helping numerous women solve their problems. These centers offer more comprehensive support compared to other phone services, which mainly provide a listening ear without the additional counseling component.

Assistance for Refugee Women

In Sarajevo, a facility dedicated to refugee women who are victims of violence was recently established. It is run by the Embassy of Local Democracy in Barcelona, an international NGO. This facility was created to address violence occurring within families and provide a haven for those affected.

Challenges with Public Services and NGO Engagement

The Centers of Social Work and public social benefits institutions have assisted vulnerable groups in Bosnia and Herzegovina. However, they often direct those seeking assistance to NGOs because they lack the resources to provide direct services. One emerging concern is the intersection of trafficking and prostitution in the region. Prostitution is illegal but carries minimal legal consequences, as it is often perceived as a voluntary choice. Lack of awareness and clear policies around trafficking compounds this issue.

While several international NGOs initially addressed violence in Bosnia and Herzegovina, many have left the region over time. One exception is the International Rescue Committee (IRC), which has implemented a comprehensive program addressing reproductive health and violence issues. IRC emphasizes grassroots initiatives and cooperation among women's NGOs and community members. The International Police Task Force (IPTF) also plays a role in addressing domestic violence, although it is not its primary focus. IPTF has initiated actions to encourage local police to deal with violence and improve their attitudes towards victims. Women's involvement in local police stations has helped enhance understanding and responsiveness.

A cocktail of Gender-based Abuses

Concentration Camp Violence and Rape

Concentration camps during the conflict in Bosnia and Herzegovina involved horrendous sexual violence. Male prisoners were forced to commit sexual assaults, rapes, and humiliations against each other. Soldiers from controlling armies also raped women in these camps. These acts of violence were intended to exert control over civilian populations, demoralize enemy armies, and disrupt communities. The mass rape of women and young girls during the war aimed to destroy families and communities by creating division and rejection within families. Organized rape was a widespread and devastating tool used throughout the conflict.

Trafficking in Women in Eastern Europe

Sexual exploitation and human trafficking have become significant criminal enterprises in Eastern and Central Europe, particularly affecting women. Trafficking often involves deception, coercion, and forced prostitution. It is estimated that over 200,000 women are trafficked annually in Eastern and Central Europe, with varying estimates for Bosnia and Herzegovina alone ranging from 4,000 to 20,000 trafficked girls and young women. Trafficking is a highly profitable business, with women being sold for thousands of German marks. Traffickers often exploit the economic hardships in source countries and the vulnerabilities of women. These are some of the key issues and responses related to domestic violence, rape, and trafficking in women in the Balkans, specifically in Bosnia and Herzegovina.

Factors Contributing to Trafficking: The post-conflict transitional regions in the Balkans and the economic and political changes in Eastern European countries have contributed to trafficking. Economic hardship, unemployment, and the breakdown of social networks in poorer countries have made women vulnerable to traffickers' false promises of job opportunities.

Challenges Faced by Trafficked Women: Rescued trafficked women and girls often face severe health issues, particularly related to reproductive health. Their exposure to sexual abuse, violence, and rape makes them highly vulnerable to sexually transmitted infections (STIs), including HIV/AIDS and unwanted pregnancies. In Bosnia and Herzegovina, trafficking often overlaps with prostitution, which is illegal but not strongly enforced. The lack of awareness about trafficking and inadequate policies poses challenges. Trafficked women often have limited access to reproductive health information and services. Many suffer from severe mental health issues, including nightmares and psychological trauma, making mental health support crucial.

Response from International Organizations

Efforts by international organizations like the International Organization for Migration (IOM) and the United Nations Population Fund (UNFPA) focus on addressing the reproductive health needs of trafficked women. They provide assistance in treating STIs, reproductive health care, counseling, and contraceptive delivery. The aim is to respond to these needs in Bosnia and Herzegovina comprehensively. International Police Task Force (IPTF) has specialized teams to combat trafficking in different regions, with efforts to increase female representation in the police force. Legal services, such as the Criminal Justice Advisory Unit (CJAU) and the International Judiciary Commission (IJC), work to protect victims and ensure proper legal procedures are followed. Police officers from various countries serving in Bosnia and Herzegovina receive training on gender violence issues. After cases of officer involvement in trafficking were reported, changes were made to the Standard Operating Procedure to strengthen measures for officers visiting establishments linked to trafficking.

Recommendations for Addressing Gender Issues in Post-Conflict Kosovo

Numerous initiatives aim to enhance access to and the quality of reproductive healthcare in post-conflict regions, and these should be specifically designed to support survivors of violence. These elements must be integrated on an equal footing with other program components.

Direct Ministry of Health in Post-Conflict Regions: UNFPA should guide the Ministry of Health in post-conflict regions to tailor programs towards victims of violence, including raising awareness among public health workers, policymakers, and decision-makers regarding the severe health consequences of violence.

Prioritize Reproductive Health Services in Shelters: UNFPA's regional programs should prioritize providing reproductive health services and improving the quality of care in shelters, making this a central objective.

Expand Counseling Services: Develop and implement counseling services at all levels of reproductive health service delivery. Additionally, integrate education on sexual and gender-based violence into population-based family planning programs.

Support NGOs Combating Violence: Extend support to non-governmental organizations (NGOs) engaged in addressing violence against both women and men. Promote networking and collaboration among these organizations.

Comprehensive Programs for Trafficked Women: Develop comprehensive programs encompassing reproductive health policies and strategies targeting trafficked women in the region, whether they are in receiving countries or their countries of origin. Implement country-specific projects.

Coordinate HIV/AIDS Testing: Collaborate with other regional agencies to coordinate HIV/AIDS testing efforts, enhancing surveillance capabilities. Promote voluntary testing through social marketing campaigns.

Consider STI Testing for UN Staff: Evaluate the feasibility of standardized procedures mandating STI testing for United Nations staff involved in efforts related to trafficking in women. Develop training and education initiatives for UN staff across the region.

Review Questions

1. Why is gender-based violence a prevalent issue in post-conflict regions?
2. What does the "empowerment approach" involve, and why is it essential in addressing gender-based violence?
3. How does violence affect both men and women in post-conflict regions, and what are the different perspectives on violence?

4. What is the role of civil society, particularly NGOs, in addressing gender-based violence in post-conflict regions?

5. What are the challenges related to reproductive health and violence in post-conflict societies?

6. How is violence against women addressed in Bosnia and Herzegovina, and what role do SOS telephone services play?

7. What factors contribute to human trafficking in Eastern and Central Europe?

8. How do international organizations respond to the issues of trafficking, domestic violence, and reproductive health in post-conflict regions?

9. What recommendations are provided for addressing gender issues in post-conflict Kosovo?

10. How can civil society and the government collaborate to combat gender-based violence effectively in post-conflict regions?

Discussion Points

1. Discuss the cultural and societal factors that contribute to gender-based violence in post-conflict regions. How do these factors vary across different regions and cultures?

2. Explore the role of international organizations and NGOs in addressing gender-based violence. What are the challenges and successes of their efforts?

3. Consider the long-term impact of gender-based violence on individuals and communities in post-conflict regions. How can societies address the physical and psychological consequences?

4. Debate the effectiveness of the empowerment approach in addressing gender-based violence. What are the advantages and disadvantages of this approach?

CHAPTER SEVEN: GENDER EQUALITY AND WOMEN'S RIGHTS IN THE AFTERMATH OF THE KOSOVO CONFLICT

Summary of Chapter Seven

1. Complex History of Kosovo: Kosovo has a complex history marked by cultural, religious, economic, and political tensions between Albanians and Serbs, with the Kosovo Conflict intensifying in the 1990s.
2. Impact of Kosovo Conflict on Women: The Kosovo Conflict had a profound impact on women, leading to their displacement, hardships, and unique challenges in a deeply patriarchal society.
3. Reproductive Health and Economic Opportunities: Efforts to address reproductive health for women, economic disparities, and challenges in the job market and the family structure.
4. Education and Violence Against Women: Challenges related to women's education, gender-based violence, and sexual abuse, and the prevalent preference for male children.
5. Minority Women and Leadership: The unique challenges faced by minority women in Kosovo, their underrepresentation in leadership positions, and the need for support from the international community.
6. Women's Role in Decision Making and Legislation: The marginaliza-

tion of women in decision-making processes, legal issues related to women's rights, and the importance of changing societal attitudes towards women.

Kosovo, a province in Southern Serbia, has a complex history marked by cultural, religious, economic, and political tensions between Albanians, who constitute the majority, and Serbs. The crisis has its roots in the fall of the Ottoman Empire and later political changes that favored Albanians but led to conflicts. Slobodan Milosevic's rise in Serbia in 1989 intensified the Kosovo Conflict, resulting in restrictions on Kosovo's autonomy and widespread expulsions of Albanians from their jobs. The 1990s witnessed the emergence of the Kosovo Liberation Army (KLA), leading to a divide among Kosovo-Albanians between advocates of peaceful methods and those who resorted to armed resistance. The conflict escalated, culminating in NATO's intervention and the eventual United Nations mission in Kosovo in 1999. Since 1999, various entities, including the UNMIK administration, United Nations agencies like UNFPA, UNIFEM, UNICEF, and international and local NGOs, have strived to collect information and assess gender-related issues in Kosovo, mainly focusing on Albanian women. Unfortunately, limited data is available regarding Serbian, Roma, and other minority women.

The mid-1990s saw the emergence of the KLA, leading to internal divisions among Kosovo-Albanians. As conflict escalated, many people, including women, were forced to flee their homes. The mass exodus to neighboring countries was marked by hardship, harassment, sexual violence against girls, and mass killings. Women, especially, were responsible for caring for their families in refugee camps. The crisis had a profound and unique impact on women in Kosovo. Traditional gender roles were deeply entrenched, with women often confined within the walls of their homes. Men dominated public life, and women's participation in policymaking and peace-building was limited. While some women engaged in grassroots activities, building NGOs and civil society, they continued to shoulder household responsibilities without male involvement. The Kosovo-Albanian population is predominantly

Muslim, and the preservation of patriarchal values posed a challenge to gender equality. Lack of respect for women was a prevailing issue rooted in historical traditions, including the legacy of the Ottoman Empire and the Kanun of Lek Dukagini.

UNFPA, along with other organizations, played a crucial role in responding to the reproductive health needs of women refugees. Contraceptives, abortion services, and maternal healthcare were provided, demonstrating the importance of addressing reproductive health in crisis settings. Despite progress and international intervention since 1999, Kosovo continues to face challenges. Economic disparities persist between urban areas and villages. High unemployment rates, limited access to healthcare, inadequate education, pollution, violence against minority groups, and trafficking in women and girls remain concerns. While some signs of reconciliation have emerged, deep-seated divisions and lingering hatred still pose challenges. The situation of women in Kosovo is complex, with deeply rooted gender disparities, but there is also resilience and hope for progress. Addressing these issues requires ongoing efforts, collaboration, and a commitment to gender equality and women's rights.

The Rise of Women Activism in Kosovo

The Kosovo crisis had profound and far-reaching effects on the lives of women in the region. Many women experienced the loss of fathers, husbands, sons, brothers, daughters, sisters, and mothers during the conflict. Alongside these personal tragedies, houses were destroyed, unemployment skyrocketed, and poverty became a grim reality for countless families. The aftermath of the crisis left Kosovo with thousands of widows who found themselves unexpectedly responsible for supporting their families, defying traditional gender roles. Conversely, some women had opportunities to travel abroad, exposing them to different cultural attitudes toward women. Upon returning to Kosovo, some of these women were motivated to work towards creating equal opportunities for their fellow women.

Despite their resilience, many women activists were shocked by the exclusion of women from decision-making processes by the male-dominated Kosovar leadership. In response, women's groups took matters into their own hands. During the 1990s, a few non-governmental organizations (NGOs) emerged alongside the Women's Forum of LDK. The Centre for Protection of Women and Children and Motrat Qiriazi, a rural women's group, were among the prominent women's NGOs. Since June 1999, numerous women's NGOs have sprung up across Kosovo, engaging in various activities to improve the welfare of women. These initiatives have included providing literacy programs for illiterate women, creating economic opportunities, offering support to widows in remote villages, and assisting traumatized women and children. The women's movement in Kosovo is diverse and robust, but these NGOs often need more support from the international community. Despite their advocacy efforts, women and women's branches of political parties face significant challenges in being heard and respected.

Economic Opportunities for Women

Before the crisis, women's participation in the Kosovar workforce lagged behind other Communist areas in Eastern Europe. In the 1970s, only 20–21 percent of the workforce consisted of women, a figure that increased only slightly to 23 percent by 1988. Several factors contributed to this, including deep-rooted traditions, the undervaluation of women's work in the agricultural sector, inadequate social services, high birth rates, and large Albanian families that often hinder women from pursuing paid employment.

Women who participated in the labor force were primarily found in education, healthcare, industry, and trade. A small number of women had received university educations. However, during the 1990s, many women lost their jobs due to the government's policy of firing Albanians. Unemployment among women in 2000 was estimated at a staggering 70 percent, higher than that of men. Most women expressed a desire to work and achieve financial independence. While the international presence created thousands of jobs and aimed for gender balance in hiring, it also introduced a new dynamic: young women becoming the primary breadwinners for their families, increasing respect and tension within households.

Unfortunately, the reduction in the presence of international NGOs, from 400 in 2000 to 200 in 2001, including United Nations agencies and UNMIK, did not significantly improve the economic situation. The slow pace of economic reconstruction, limited programs to create economic opportunities for women, and insufficient funding were persistent challenges. Notably, UNIFEM had to cancel its "Economic Opportunities for Women" project due to financial constraints despite the clear need for such initiatives, particularly concerning Kosovo's demographic structure, characterized by many widows and young women of working age. However, some positive developments occurred. The international community's official policy of hiring equal numbers of women and men whenever possible provided job opportunities for many women. This policy also gave rise to a new phenomenon in Kosovar society: young women becoming the primary providers for their families. While this challenged traditional gender roles and norms, it raised questions about societal acceptance of this evolving family structure.

The economic opportunities available to women in Kosovo were significantly affected by the conflict and its aftermath. Job losses, increased dependence among married women, limited economic opportunities, and the challenges faced by large families and inadequate social services all hindered women's access to paid work. However, educated women did find new opportunities through the United Nations mission, and there were signs of improved access to education for women, which promised better prospects in the future.

Women and Education

Traditionally, women in Kosovo had lower levels of education compared to men. Estimates suggested an illiteracy rate of 10-15 percent among women and 2-3 percent among men, although these figures were subject to debate. More comprehensive research was needed to establish reliable data. During the 1990s, Belgrade's policies had severe consequences for women's education in Kosovo. The Kosovo-Albanians operated a "Parallel System" of education during this period, running schools at all levels but with limited resources, which resulted in an entire generation (1989-1999) receiving education that fell below European standards and required improvement. Security concerns during the 1990s led many parents to keep their daughters from attending school, resulting in high dropout rates among girls.

The Kosovo Common Assessment 2000 indicated that many teenage girls, particularly in rural areas, had never attended or completed secondary school. Girls dropped out as early as age 13, often due to family priorities and economic constraints. In 1999, only 20-25 percent of young people aged 19-24 continued their education beyond lower levels. Although the gender gap in higher education has narrowed over the years, women still face significant barriers. Kosovo-Albanian women reported that many parents in rural areas considered education for girls unnecessary, preferring to prioritize their sons' education due to limited family resources. In 1989, women constituted only 33.5 percent of students at the University of Pristina. While progress had been made in closing the gender gap, there remained room for improvement. Kosovo urgently needed various training and retraining programs to bridge the education gap and introduce new ideas and techniques. Many individuals found it difficult and humiliating to return to school after gaps in their education. The concept of "lifelong learning" needed to be introduced and promoted. s called for new curricula, teaching methods, better standards, improved access to education, and the recognition of the equal right to education for all.

Women's Reproductive Health and Reproductive Rights

Kosovo-Albanian women emphasized work, education, health, and reproductive health as the most critical issues facing women. Maternal mortality rates were high, with approximately 20 percent of pregnant women delivering their babies outside healthcare facilities and 17 percent receiving no assistance from trained professionals during childbirth. Kosovo had a high birth rate of 2.7, among the highest in Europe, with short intervals between births. Despite these challenges, access to contraceptives was limited, requiring visits to specialists or healthcare centers, often located far from communities. Condom distribution campaigns aimed to encourage their use, but discussions about contraceptives remained taboo in Kosovo's culture, with resistance stemming from historical mistrust of family planning efforts by the Serbian regime.

Abortions were legal in Kosovo, but the frequency remained unknown. An indication of the sex ratio at birth, higher than the natural population equilibrium, suggested possible selective abortion practices. Low contraceptive use, combined with an average fertility rate of 2.8 children per woman in 1999, suggested the widespread use of abortion for fertility control. Excessive abortions contributed to high infant and maternal mortality rates. Little information was available about breastfeeding practices, but its absence might partially explain the poor health of newborns.

Furthermore, the consequences of child loss on the health of mothers remained largely unexplored. Women's overall health in Kosovo was poor, with high rates of anemia, smoking, and trauma stemming from the conflict. Traumatized women, particularly in areas of intense fighting and disappearances, continued to face mental health challenges and difficulties adapting to a new future. Sexual orientation remained a cultural taboo, and many LGBTQ+ individuals concealed their sexuality due to societal pressures.

Trafficking in Women

One of the earliest issues addressed by international agencies and NGOs in Kosovo was the trafficking of women. Within just three months of the international presence, it became evident that this was a growing problem. A Gender Task Force Meeting, organized by UNIFEM resulted in the development of the UNMIK Regulation on trafficking in persons, which the United Nations later approved. Kosovo, once a transit route for traffickers, had become a destination point and a new market for the sex trade. Despite efforts by KFOR, police, and international agencies to combat trafficking, challenges persisted. Women were moved frequently to evade authorities, new clubs and brothels continuously opened, and corruption facilitated the operations. While evidence of women being trafficked out of Kosovo was limited, there was ongoing concern about the number of women who had died or were unable to return to their home countries.

Reports indicated that a significant number of victims were young women, trafficked mainly from Bulgaria, the Republic of Moldova, Romania, and Ukraine. Many of them were 18-24 years old, living with their families, with limited access to healthcare, and low condom use. Shockingly, it was reported that 70-80 percent of "clients" were Kosovo-Albanians, with 20-30 percent being international staff members. Efforts to combat trafficking included campaigns to raise awareness about its dangers, implications, and the responsibility of the broader community. Calls were made for an international Code of Conduct prohibiting international agency workers in Kosovo from purchasing sex, although enforcement remained challenging.

Violence against Women

Violence against women was a pervasive but hidden problem in Kosovo. After the crisis, increased attention was given to violence against women, including domestic violence and trafficking. However, discussing domestic violence was relatively new in Kosovo, and there was resistance to acknowledging its extent. International and local lawyers debated the inclusion of domestic violence in the Penal Code, with some arguing it was a private matter and not the concern of the public. Although there were ongoing efforts to address this issue, work on the Penal Code remained incomplete at the time. Kosovo-Albanian women reported that violence against women was on the rise. However, due to a lack of pre-conflict data, it was challenging to determine whether this resulted from increased incidents or greater awareness and reporting. The problem extended to violence by partners and family members, with 23 percent of women surveyed disclosing that they had experienced violence. Additionally, 18 percent reported rape by a partner or family member, figures comparable to other countries. Further research was needed to understand better the extent of rape, sexual abuse, and violence against young girls.

The Girl Child

The topic of violence against children and sexual abuse was still taboo, with many women unwilling to discuss it. Nevertheless, there were concerns about the prevalence of violence against children, particularly girls, and the urgent need for more research on this issue. Reports suggested that teachers used physical violence, such as beating pupils, though there were discussions about banning such practices. Kosovo preferred male children, reflected in a male/female birth ratio that favored boys. This preference extended to families, where boys were often more enthusiastically welcomed than girls. Abandoned babies at Pristina Hospital, predominantly girls, highlighted this preference, as it was more challenging to find families willing to adopt girls. Girls in Kosovo faced barriers to education and fewer opportunities compared to boys. Girls were often burdened with time-consuming household chores from an early age, unlike boys. This difference in expectations contributed to disparities in access to education and opportunities.

Minority Women

Kosovo's minority population, estimated at around 200,000, faced unique challenges. Isolation, insecurity, high unemployment, poverty, restricted freedom of movement, violence against women and children, and limited access to social services were among the problems affecting minority women. which was particularly pronounced among Roma women, who experienced high birth and maternal mortality rates, early marriages, limited education, and economic opportunities. Serbian women, while generally better educated, faced difficulties due to the broader challenges affecting minorities, as they were often viewed as collectively responsible for the actions of the Serb-dominated Yugoslav government during the 1990s conflicts. Trauma, pessimism, anger, and a lack of hope were prevalent among minority women, many of whom were internally displaced in Kosovo. Support from the international community remained insufficient. Despite the presence of powerful women among minority groups, leadership positions were typically held by men, leaving minority women underrepresented. Additionally, there were no gender-based programs or activities for teenagers in Kosovo, which led to challenges for both girls and boys in terms of opportunities and safety.

In summary, Kosovo faced a range of gender-related challenges in the aftermath of the conflict, including violence against women, trafficking, unequal access to education and opportunities for girls, and unique difficulties faced by minority women. Addressing these issues required comprehensive efforts and continued research to understand better and tackle the root causes of gender disparities and violence in the region.

Women and Decision-Making: Women in Politics

Historically, women in Kosovo have been marginalized in decision-making processes and societal shaping, facing significant economic, social, and cultural challenges. These obstacles have limited their ability to address these issues effectively, as they have been excluded from decision-making roles. Consequently, women remain underrepresented in various governing bodies, including the UNMIK "government" and other reconstructive institutions. For example, among the 20 local leaders in the Joint Interim Administrative Structures, only two are women. While there has been some progress in including women in the Kosovo Transitional Council, where six women (16.2 percent), primarily representing civil society, serve as advisory members, this achievement resulted from significant pressure from local and international women's groups. Most of the women elected to municipal councils belong to the LDK party, and although they play essential roles in addressing local government issues, few hold leadership positions.

Kosovo has seen the emergence of a network of Albanian women's NGOs and groups in recent years, with many demonstrating strong leadership and efforts to empower women. The Women's Coalition, formed by multiple NGOs, political parties, and media outlets, aimed to increase women's representation and participation in political and economic life. Despite initial campaigns, their success could have been improved, and internal conflicts within the coalition hampered progress. Tensions persisted between some women's NGOs and women's branches of political parties, highlighting the need for solidarity and collaboration in empowering women within Kosovo's predominantly male-dominated society.

Legislation, Human Rights, and Women's Protection

Upon the arrival of UNMIK, one of the initial challenges was to identify existing laws and establish procedures for creating new legislation in Kosovo. Existing Yugoslav Republic legislation technically granted women "equal rights," but these rights were often not upheld or respected by the Kosovo-Albanian community. Although women in Kosovo have the right to vote and run for elections, there were instances during local elections where men insisted on voting on behalf of their wives, claiming that women were incapable of voting. Female candidates received minimal support during these elections. While divorce is legally possible, it becomes more challenging when children are involved, as Kosovo-Albanian society places a strong emphasis on family unity. Traditionally, women do not retain custody of their children after divorce or the death of their husbands; instead, children are considered part of the husband's family. This tradition makes it difficult for women to leave abusive marriages. Kosovo lacks legislation promoting equal opportunities for women and men and comprehensive programs in various departments and municipalities.

Women's labor rights still need improvements. For instance, women will want more secure rights, including extended maternity leave periods, than the Yugoslav Republic's regulations. Enhancing reproductive rights legislation, including access to contraceptives, healthcare, sex education, and resources, is critical. Additionally, robust domestic violence legislation is needed to safeguard women and children. Kosovo's Legal Framework, established in 2001, requires the new government to implement the Convention on the Elimination of All Forms of Discrimination against Women (CEDAW), allowing women to advocate for their rights. However, the Convention on the Rights of the Child is not explicitly mentioned in this framework. Although a Kosovo Action Plan for the Advancement of Women was being developed under the

UNMIK Office of Gender Affairs, it faced challenges due to disagreements and misunderstandings about UNMIK's role versus local authority. Substantial legislative reforms are necessary, but even more so, a change in societal attitudes towards women and their human rights is required. Campaigns and public education efforts are essential to raise awareness about women's pivotal role in shaping society and their rights to instigate change.

Women and the Role of the Family

In Kosovo, the extended family has historically held great importance, similar to other parts of Europe during the Middle Ages. Respect for family duties, including protection, provision of food and shelter, and the pursuit of justice for harmed family members, remains deeply rooted. While changes are happening, these values remain significant in Kosovo-Albanian society, which highly regards large families as blessings. Marriage customs also reflect these traditions. After marriage, women often move in with their parents-in-law and are expected to partake in household responsibilities, whether they hold paid employment or not. Inadequate social services, including childcare and support for disabled individuals and seniors, place the onus on families, primarily women, to provide these services. While arranged marriages persist in rural areas, nuclear families are on the rise in larger towns. Among Serbs, nuclear families dominate, and children often attend boarding schools, especially for university education.

Gender Issues and Peacekeeping Missions

The United Nations, through various conventions and resolutions like CEDAW, the Beijing Platform for Action, Beijing +5 Platform for Action, and Resolution 1325 on Women and Peace, emphasizes eliminating discrimination against women, promoting equal opportunities for women and men, and addressing gender-related concerns during peacekeeping missions. UNMIK, international organizations, and NGOs have played significant roles in Kosovo's reconstruction, aiming to raise gender awareness and tackle issues affecting women. Despite some progress, gender perspectives have not been consistently integrated into policymaking and programs. UNMIK's Office of Gender Affairs lacks the necessary authority, resources, and trained staff to exert the required influence. Training for gender focal points and gender-sensitive training for all staff members remain underutilized. Gender mainstreaming within policies and programs is inadequate, and international staff members often lack an understanding of gender-related concepts. The lack of gender sensitivity among senior staff members poses a significant obstacle to gender mainstreaming.

Peacekeeping missions should emphasize information sharing, the gathering of sex-disaggregated data, cultural analysis, and gender sensitization and training for all staff members. Programs must be developed with a gender perspective, agencies should establish equal opportunity policies, and gender focal points should be appointed where applicable. In addition, local women's involvement should be prioritized, and their needs and demands should be assessed and supported.

Lessons Learned on Reproductive Health

Efforts to address reproductive health should consider using the media for sex education and raising awareness. Engaging with local politicians to promote women's reproductive rights through legislation and policies is crucial. Collaboration with women's NGOs and community education initiatives should be undertaken, emphasizing campaigns and discussions to destigmatize reproductive health issues. Support from donors and other United Nations organizations and agencies is necessary for these programs to succeed, given the importance of reproductive health in reducing poverty, improving lives, promoting gender equality, and empowering women.

In summary, the Kosovo conflict had severe consequences for women and girls, limiting their freedom, education, and economic prospects. Many women became refugees, experiencing trauma and loss. However, women's NGOs were vital in supporting them during these difficult times. Reconstruction efforts led by UNMIK, OSCE, and the EU brought new challenges, with continued unemployment and poverty. Women assumed critical roles as breadwinners for their families, and women's NGOs received support from international partners. Several issues, including illiteracy, limited access to education, unemployment, lack of social services, high birth rates, maternal mortality, health problems, domestic violence, and trafficking in women, persist. Women remain underrepresented in positions of power and decision-making. Cultural taboos and societal challenges make discussing these issues difficult. Efforts to integrate gender perspectives and mainstreaming have fallen short of United Nations policies. Improvements require better cooperation, data gathering, cultural understanding, gender sensitization, and local women's involvement in all aspects of peacekeeping missions. Kosovo offers valuable lessons for future missions to address gender disparities effectively.

Review Questions

1. What historical events contributed to the Kosovo Conflict, and how did it impact women in the region?
2. How did women in Kosovo adapt to their changing roles as breadwinners for their families during and after the conflict?
3. What were the primary factors that hindered women's participation in the Kosovar workforce before and after the conflict?
4. What challenges did girls face in accessing education and opportunities in Kosovo, and why did the gender gap persist?
5. How did the conflict affect reproductive health and reproductive rights for women in Kosovo?
6. What were the key concerns and challenges in addressing trafficking in women in Kosovo?
7. How did cultural and societal norms affect the discussion of violence against women and children in Kosovo?

8. What role did international peacekeeping missions play in addressing gender issues in Kosovo, and what were the limitations of these efforts?

Discussion Points

1. The role of women's NGOs in Kosovo's post-conflict recovery and their struggle for recognition and support.
2. The impact of economic disparities and unemployment on women in Kosovo and their evolving role as primary breadwinners.
3. The role of cultural and societal norms in shaping the gender landscape in Kosovo and the challenges in changing these norms.
4. The need for international cooperation and support in addressing gender-related issues in post-conflict regions like Kosovo.

CHAPTER EIGHT: SMALL ARMS REGULATION AND ITS IMPACT ON GENDER VIOLENCE IN SOUTH AFRICA

Summary of Chapter Eight

1. Firearms Control Act and Gender-Based Violence: The Firearms Control Act (FCA) was enacted in South Africa in 2000, partly in response to a tragic incident involving a registered gun owner who killed his family. The FCA empowered law enforcement agencies to remove firearms from individuals involved in domestic violence, demonstrating the Act's potential impact on individuals' lives.

2. Gender Violence and Small Arms: South Africa faces high rates of gender-based violence (GBV), including a significant female homicide rate and widespread GBV. The misuse of firearms plays a role in this violence, particularly in intimate partner femicides and violence against LGBTQ+ individuals.

3. Post-Apartheid Law-Making: South Africa's firearms legislation was developed during the post-apartheid era, characterized by collaboration, inclusivity, and a focus on the collective good rather than individual rights. Prominent women and civil society representatives were crucial in shaping firearms control policies.

4. Global and Regional Influences: Global, regional, and national developments influenced South Africa's firearms legislation. The UN

Firearms Protocol, the Southern Africa Development Community's (SADC) Firearms Protocol, and successful gun control movements in Canada, the UK, and Australia all played a role in shaping South Africa's policies.

5. Crafting and Implementing the FCA: South Africa's firearms legislation development process involved collaboration between government and civil society. While there was resistance to gender-sensitive measures, advocacy by women's groups and alliances within the ANC led to the inclusion of some safeguards for women.

6. Impact on Firearm-Related Deaths and Ownership: The FCA initially led to a decline in gun homicides, particularly intimate femicides. However, a subsequent breakdown in enforcement and governance led to increased firearm availability, contributing to a recent surge in firearm-related violence.

Gender and Small Arms Policymaking in South Africa

In June 2000, shortly before South Africa's parliament adopted the Firearms Control Act (FCA), a tragic incident occurred when police inspector Jeffery Sampson, a registered gun owner, shot and killed his wife, lover, and two young children before taking his own life. This event highlighted the urgent need for stricter firearms control. Over 15 years later, in 2016, Gun Free South Africa (GFSA), a national NGO, assisted a woman named Lucille in reporting her husband's history of violence and abuse to the police. This report aimed to demonstrate that her husband was not "fit and proper" to possess a firearm, resulting in the denial of his competency certificate, the first step in applying for a firearm license. Lucille's case exemplifies how legislation like the FCA, when properly implemented and defended, can have tangible effects on individuals' lives.

The enactment of the FCA occurred during a significant social and political transformation in South Africa, marked by the end of apartheid. This transition led to the introduction of progressive laws, including a new constitution (1996) and legislation addressing women's concerns and well-being, such as the Choice on Termination of Pregnancy Act of 1996 and the Domestic Violence Act (DVA) of 1998. Elements of the FCA also reflected this gender focus by considering domestic violence incidents as grounds for firearm license refusal. The Act also empowered courts and law enforcement agencies to remove firearms from individuals misusing them, particularly in cases of domestic violence. Additionally, the DVA allowed women to report the presence of firearms in domestic violence incidents or when seeking domestic violence protection orders at magistrates' courts.

Gender, Violence, and Guns

South Africa stands out among non-conflict-affected countries for its high prevalence of lethal violence against women and girls, including a high female homicide rate, widespread sexual and gender-based violence (GBV), and a significant cost associated with GBV. These issues are exacerbated by socioeconomic inequality, cultural norms that accept violence, weak law enforcement, and the exposure of children to violence, leading to a cycle of violence. Gun use and violence in South Africa have complex gender dimensions. While the majority of legal gun owners are men, most firearms are registered for self-defense purposes, and men over the age of 50 years constitute the largest demographic of gun owners. Nevertheless, most gun violence victims are young black men living in urban areas and victimized by other young black men using illegal firearms. The primary source of illegal guns is the theft or loss of licensed firearms, averaging 24 such incidents daily. Despite women constituting only 11 percent of gun-related murder victims, firearms play a significant role in violence against women (VAW), especially in intimate partner femicides. Firearms also play a role in violence against LGBTQ+ individuals, with hate crimes disproportionately affecting this community.

Law-making in South Africa post-1994: the early days

South Africa's firearms legislation was enacted during the post-apartheid democratic era, characterized by the promulgation of numerous laws. The process involved substantial input from civil society organizations, research institutions, and grassroots participation. The approach was collaborative and prioritized the public good over individual rights. In the years leading up to the FCA, the government initiated several committees to address the proliferation of firearms. These committees, which included prominent women and civil society representatives, played a crucial role in shaping the discourse and policy solutions related to firearm control. This engagement disrupted the traditional male-dominated discourse on firearms, emphasizing the collective good and leading to more inclusive policies.

Global, Regional, and National Developments Before and After the FCA

Several global, regional, and national developments influenced South Africa's firearms legislation. The UN Firearms Protocol, negotiated concurrently with the FCA, adopted a law-enforcement approach to control firearms. Regionally, the Southern Africa Development Community's (SADC) Firearms Protocol reinforced South Africa's efforts to implement the FCA rigorously, aligning it with neighboring countries' more restrictive firearm legislation. Notably, these protocols lacked gender-specific provisions.

Nationally, influential gun control movements in Canada, the UK, and Australia prompted policy changes. In Canada, background checks included spousal interviews to reduce the risk of violence against women. The UK and Australia also implemented firearm control measures following large-scale massacres. In all these cases, women-led alliances and civil society played pivotal roles in advocating for legislative reform. Additionally, the UN Program of Action to Prevent, Combat, and Eradicate the Illicit Trade in Small Arms and Light Weapons (PoA) placed firearm related violence and the need to reduce the supply, demand, and availability of illicit guns at the forefront of global small arms policies. The PoA recognized the role of civil society in small arms policy development, paving the way for discussions on the gendered nature and impacts of firearm-related violence.

Crafting, Passing, and Implementing the FCA

In South Africa, policy development is orchestrated by the executive branch within the relevant department. New laws are typically initiated in response to identified issues that necessitate policy or legislative solutions. The domain of firearms control policy falls under the Ministry of Police, and the Civilian Secretariat for Police (CSP) plays a pivotal role in steering the policy process with a strong focus on human-centric security. In 2000, while the Firearms Control Bill was under discussion in parliament, the CSP provided crucial baseline data on firearm-related crime, notably including statistics on gun-related deaths. Policy formulation in South Africa follows two essential steps: the Green Paper, a preliminary policy document for public input, and the White Paper, which represents the final policy position. While the formal processes were not strictly adhered to, the policy committee report, along with the CSP's data, effectively served as the basis for the government's final stance on firearms control, akin to a White Paper.

The Firearms Control Bill, approved by the cabinet, was published in late 1999 and presented to parliament in May 2000. During this period, the public was invited to submit written comments, leading to over 3,000 submissions, indicating significant public interest. Additionally, 93 oral submissions were made during public hearings in mid-2000. While firearm owners, predominantly white men, dominated the hearings, the Gun Control Alliance (GCA), representing diverse groups, including public health experts, researchers, religious communities, and young people from violence-affected communities, contributed significantly.

During the final review of the Bill by the Portfolio Committee for Police (PCoP), there was resistance, even within the African National Congress

(ANC), to include language-strengthening protections for women in their homes, including reluctance to legislate interim protection orders as sufficient grounds for denying gun certificate applications. The GCA supported influential women within the ANC's women's caucus and the sole member of parliament from a minority party in the PCoP, providing them with examples of best practices globally and regionally, as well as national data illustrating the risks faced by women at home. This advocacy resulted in the inclusion of some measures to safeguard women, although only some of the complete set of proposals. The prevailing cultural norms within the legislative sphere, emphasizing that the private domain should remain unlegislated, influenced this outcome.

Effects on Firearm-Related Deaths and Firearm Ownership

Over nearly two decades in South Africa, the development and implementation of small arms control policies revealed a discernible pattern. Initially, there was a high incidence of gun homicides during apartheid and the early years of democracy, followed by a sustained decline over a decade during full FCA implementation. However, this trend started to reverse in 2011, coinciding with decreased state accountability, effective governance, administrative efficiency, and the state's capacity to enforce the law. This lapse in enforcement led to increased firearm availability.

Examining gender-specific impacts, the FCA contributed to a significant reduction in firearm-related intimate femicides from 1999 to 2009. A ten-year retrospective study indicated a decline in women killed by their intimate partners, dropping from four women per day in 1999 to three per day in 2009, primarily due to a reduction in firearm-related fatalities. The recent surge in firearm-related violence can be attributed to the breakdown of the national firearms control system. Poor enforcement and compliance have led to an increased availability of firearms. For example, 33% of licensed firearm owners failed to renew their licenses in 2015–16, yet these firearms remained in their possession. The firearms management system has also faced fraud, corruption, inadequate stockpile management, under-resourcing, and a lack of policing capacity. An alarming illustration of this failure was the case of an ex-police colonel who, responsible for managing firearms destined for destruction, stole 2,000 firearms and sold them to gang leaders, resulting in the tragic deaths of 89 children. Another noteworthy case is that of Lucille, whose husband, despite being initially denied a gun certificate due to her testimony, later successfully appealed and obtained a license. This outcome was likely due to inadequate record-keeping and broader failures within the criminal justice system, including delays in obtaining domestic protection orders, with local courts infrequently ordering the police to confiscate firearms.

The South African experience with crafting and implementing small arms control policies offers valuable insights for addressing gun violence and gender-based violence (GBV) in other countries. South African policymakers and advocates seized upon a pivotal moment—the end of apartheid—to push for progressive policies, particularly regarding civilian firearm possession. This endeavor faced organized opposition stemming from deep historical and cultural connections to firearm ownership, especially among white men. The change in political dynamics, however, placed white men on equal footing with other interest groups in the policymaking process.

A positive aspect of this journey is the growing influence of women's meaningful participation and leadership in an area traditionally dominated by men. South Africa has moved closer to a situation where all affected parties can contribute to shaping policies that enhance safety and security for everyone.

Review Questions

1. How did a tragic incident involving a registered gun owner impact firearms control in South Africa?
2. What are the key factors contributing to the high prevalence of gender-based violence in South Africa?
3. How did the post-apartheid era influence the development of firearms

control policies in South Africa?

4. What were the global and regional influences on South Africa's firearms legislation?

5. How did women's groups and alliances within the ANC contribute to including gender-sensitive measures in the Firearms Control Act?

6. What were the initial effects of the Firearms Control Act on firearm-related deaths in South Africa?

7. What factors led to a reversal in the decline of gun homicides in South Africa in recent years?

8. What challenges have been faced in enforcing firearms control policies in South Africa?

Discussion Points

1. The role of women's groups and alliances in influencing firearms control policies: Discuss the significance of women's involvement in shaping policies that impact gender-based violence and gun control in South Africa.

2. Lessons for other countries: Explore the lessons that can be drawn from South Africa's experience with firearms control, particularly in addressing gun violence and gender-based violence.

3. The challenges of enforcing firearms control: Analyze the factors contributing to the breakdown of enforcement and governance, leading to increased firearm availability and violence.

4. Gender-sensitive policies and their impact: Discuss the effectiveness of gender-sensitive measures in reducing gender-based violence, including intimate partner femicides, and their relevance in other regions.

CONCLUSION

As we conclude the book "Firearms, Gender Violence, and the Pursuit of Equality," it is essential to reflect on the transformative power of knowledge, the need for collective action, and the unyielding spirit of hope that lights our path. From the first to the eighth Chapter, the harsh realities of gender-based violence as a pressing global challenge are discussed. Chapter One reveals that about 30% of women worldwide have experienced physical and sexual violence. Firearms, often wielded as instruments of terror, stand as ominous symbols of the vulnerability that so many women endure, even within the walls of their own homes.

The "gun culture" casts shadows over gender equality, underscoring the inextricable link between societal memories, insecurity, and the perpetuation of violence. The international frameworks support gender-conscious firearms control. However, action towards achieving it is scarce, indicating a wide gap between intent and implementation. The Serbian case study demonstrates how well-established legal frameworks and regulations coexist with the need for improved enforcement and greater gender sensitivity.

Chapter Two illuminated the shadowy world of illicit small arms and light weapons, a daunting threat to international security, which necessitates not just national legislation but also the fortification of criminal justice systems. The significance of international cooperation and information-sharing was starkly evident, emphasizing the pivotal role of international agreements like the United Nations Convention against Transnational Organized Crime and its Firearms Protocol. The Chapter equally unveiled the indispensable nature of gender-responsive small-arms programming and the profound influence of gender analysis.

Chapter Three explained the MOSAIC, the Modular Small-Arms-Control Implementation Compendium, a potent tool in the fight against the illicit trade and misuse of SALW. The development of MOSAIC represented the convergence of twenty-four partner entities, resulting in a voluntary toolkit that aligns with global agreements, notably the Sustainable Development Goals. This Chapter drew attention to the intrinsic connections between gender equality and the reduction of illicit arms flows, demonstrating the indispensability of addressing the gender perspective in small arms and light weapons control. Gender mainstreaming assumed the central role of ensuring that small-arms control initiatives considered the multifaceted consequences of their actions. This process demanded a comprehensive understanding of the disparate impacts of small arms on men and women, particularly as they pertained to masculinity, small arms, and violence.

Chapter Four exposed the intricate balance between their effectiveness and challenges, shaping a clearer understanding of their role in reducing the presence of small arms and light weapons in conflict zones. In Chapter Five, we honed in on the central role of governments and civil society in small arms and light weapons control. The critical role of donors in supporting national SALW control efforts, particularly in low-income and post-conflict settings, was underscored in Chapter Five. This Chapter also offered insights into the eight-point agenda for gender equality in crisis prevention, encapsulated by the United Nations Development Program (UNDP), underscoring the comprehensive nature of gender equality advocacy.

Chapter Six transported us to post-conflict regions, where the scourge of gender-based violence persisted, deeply rooted in the historical acceptance of violence against women as a societal norm. As we delved into the empowerment approach, the significance of challenging power structures and understanding the ubiquity of violence became clear. Civil society, particularly non-governmental organizations, emerged as a critical force in filling the gaps left by government efforts. Reproductive health and society assumed central positions in our discussion, emphasizing the challenges faced by post-conflict regions, including inadequate reproductive health education and limited access to contraceptives. In the case of Bosnia and Herzegovina, we discovered the pivotal role of SOS telephone services and non-governmental organizations in providing support to victims of family violence.

In Chapter Seven, the complex history of Kosovo unfolded, marked by cultural, religious, economic, and political tensions. The profound impact of the Kosovo Conflict on women became evident as we explored their displacement, hardships, and unique struggles in a deeply patriarchal society. This Chapter exposed efforts to address reproductive health, economic disparities, and challenges in the job market and the family structure. The inescapable realities of gender-based violence and sexual abuse were juxtaposed with the enduring preference for male children. Minority women in Kosovo, marginalized and underrepresented in leadership positions, emerged as voices needing support from the international community.

Lastly, Chapter Eight presents the South African case, a nation that grapples with the misuse of firearms in the context of gender-based violence. The Firearms Control Act (FCA), introduced in 2000, emerged as a potent symbol of change, empowered to intervene in domestic violence and enhance the safety of individuals' lives. South Africa's history of post-apartheid law-making illuminated the profound role of collaboration, inclusivity, and a focus on the collective good in shaping firearms control policies. We were reminded of the global and regional influences that shaped South Africa's firearms legislation, revealing the profound impact of international agreements and successful gun control movements in other countries. The impact of the FCA on firearm-related deaths and ownership in South Africa was a sobering reminder of the ongoing challenges.

As we conclude this book, it is essential to note that there are still more questions than answers, for the pursuit of equality, is a relentless quest shaped by the resilience of those who dare to dream of a world unburdened by the weight of gender-based violence. We hope that the chapters within this book serve not as the end of the journey but as the beginning of a profound commitment—a commitment to engage, challenge, and act. It is our collective responsibility to strive for a future where the pursuit of equality is no longer a battle but an enduring truth.

AREAS FOR FURTHER RESEARCH AND STUDIES

The journey through "Firearms, Gender Violence, and the Pursuit of Equality" has touched upon a wide array of topics, each shedding light on the complex dynamics of gender-based violence, small arms control, and gender equality. To delve deeper into these critical areas, scholars, policymakers, activists, and curious minds can explore the following avenues for further reading and research:

1. Firearm Ownership, Domestic Violence, and Gender Equality:

- Research the challenges of implementing international frameworks that address gender aspects of firearms control.
- Examine the effectiveness of legal frameworks and regulations related to firearm ownership in different countries.
- Investigate the psychological and sociological factors contributing to the "gun culture" and insecurity in regions like Serbia.
- Small Arms Control and Organized Crime:
- Study the implementation and effectiveness of national legislation controlling small arms and light weapons.
- Explore the role of international cooperation in combating organized crime's access to firearms, focusing on the United Nations Convention against Transnational Organized Crime and its Firearms Protocol.
- Analyze the multi-dimensional connections between small arms control, human rights, counter-terrorism, peacekeeping, and development.

2. Gender-Responsive Strategies for SALW Governance:

- Investigate the roles and effectiveness of governmental and civil society organizations in promoting gender equality and local ownership of small arms and light weapons.
- Explore the impact of regional organizations in addressing cross-border challenges related to SALW.
- Examine the extent to which the UN and its coordinating mechanisms, such as the UN Coordinating Action on Small Arms (CASA), incorporate gender considerations into their initiatives.

3. Gender-Based Violence in Post-Conflict Regions:

- Research the prevalence and consequences of gender-based violence in various post-conflict regions, considering cultural norms and historical contexts.
- Study the effectiveness of empowerment approaches for challenging established power structures and fostering gender equality.
- Investigate the challenges and opportunities in providing reproductive health education and services in post-conflict areas.

4. Gender Equality and Women's Rights After Conflict:

- Explore the impact of conflicts on women's roles in decision-making processes and leadership positions.
- Analyze efforts to address economic disparities, education, and violence against women in post-conflict settings.
- Investigate the role of the international community in supporting minority women and challenging societal attitudes towards women in the aftermath of conflict.

5. Small Arms Regulation and Its Impact on Gender Violence:

- Study the impact of firearms control legislation, like the Firearms Control Act (FCA) in South Africa, on gender-based violence and intimate partner femicides.
- Examine the development and implementation of post-apartheid firearms legislation in South Africa, with a focus on the role of women's groups and civil society.
- Research the global and regional influences that have shaped firearms control policies in different countries.

6. Cross-Cutting Themes:

- Investigate the intersections of gender with other identity markers, such as race, class, and sexual orientation, in the context of gender-based violence and small arms control.
- Explore the impact of climate change, migration, and conflict on gender dynamics and the prevalence of firearms.
- Study innovative methodologies and research tools to advance gender-responsive research in the fields of small arms control and gender-based violence.

These areas of further reading and research offer a deeper understanding of the multifaceted issues explored in the book, with the potential to inform policy decisions, advocacy efforts, and academic discourse on these critical matters.

SOURCES

Gender And Small Arms Control UNODA https://disarmament.unoda.org/gender-and-small-arms-control/

Militarizing Gender or Humanizing Small Arms Control? October 13, 2022by Callum Watson IPI Global observatory https://theglobalobservatory.org/2022/10/militarizing-gender-or-humanizing-small-arms-control/

Gender Brief for UNODC Staff Mainstreaming gender in Organized Crime & Illicit Trafficking projects https://www.unodc.org/documents/Gender/Thematic_Gender_Briefs_English/Org_crime_and_trafficking_brief_23_03_2020.pdf

brief 24 Gender Perspectives on Small Arms and Light Weapons: Regional and International Concerns BONN International Center For Conversion https://www.bicc.de/uploads/tx_bicctools/brief24.pdf

Arms control OSCE https://www.osce.org/arms-control

Small Arms, Light Weapons and Landmines Camille Pampell Conaway https://www.inclusivesecurity.org/wp-content/uploads/2012/04/48_small_arms.pdf

Inclusive Security, Sustainable Peace: A Toolkit For Advocacy and Action Security Issues

Women, Gender and DDR UN 2006 https://www.unddr.org/modules/IDDRS-5.10-Women-Gender-and-DDR.pdf

Global Governance To Address Proliferation Of Small Arms And Light Weapons To Prevent Armed Conflicts And Promote Peace https://ideasforpeace.org/content/global-governance-to-address-proliferation-of-small-arms-and-light-weapons/

Facts and figures: Women, peace, and security https://www.unwomen.org/en/what-we-do/peace-and-security/facts-and-figures

Integrating Gender in Post-Conflict Security Sector Reform Megan Bastick Geneva Centre for the Democratic Control of Armed Forces (DCAF) Policy Paper – №29 https://www.dcaf.ch/sites/default/files/publications/documents/pp29.pdf

Gender, War & Peacebuilding A Study Guide Series On Peace And Conflict For Independent Learners And Classroom Instructors https://www.usip.org/sites/default/files/files/NPECSG12.pdf

The Impact of Armed Conflict on Women and Girls A Consultative Meeting on Mainstreaming Gender in Areas of Conflict and Reconstruction Bratislava, Slovakia 13–15 November 2001 UNFPABratislava, Slovakia 13-15 November 2002 https://www.unfpa.org/sites/default/files/pub-pdf/impact_conflict_women.pdf

Modular Small-Arms-Control Implementation Compendium MOSAIC 03.30 2018 https://iansa.org/wp-content/uploads/2021/04/MOSAIC-03.30-2015E V1.0.pdf

NATO Guidelines for Gender Mainstreaming in Small Arms & Light Weapons Projects https://salw.hq.nato.int/Content/resources/NGforGM_EN_Small%20Arms.pdf

Gender Brief for UNODC Staff Mainstreaming gender in Organized Crime & Illicit Trafficking Projects https://www.unodc.org/documents/Gender/Thematic_Gender_Briefs_English/Org_crime_and_trafficking_brief_23_03_2020.pdf

Preventing Gender-Based Violence Through Arms Control: Tools and guidelines to implement the Arms Trade Treaty and UN Programme of Action 2016 Reaching Critical Will of the Women's International League for Peace and Freedom https://att-assistance.org/sites/default/files/2019-01/rcw_att-unpoa-gender-based-violence.pdf

Small arms and light weapons - Report of the Secretary-General (S/2021/839) [EN/AR/RU/ZH] 30 Sep 2021 https://reliefweb.int/report/world/small-arms-and-light-weapons-report-secretary-general-s2021839-enarruzh

Gender-responsive Small Arms Control A Practical Guide Edited by Emile Le-Brun Small Arms Survey, Graduate Institute of International and Development Studies, Geneva 2019 Small Arms Survey **https://smallarmssurvey.org/sites/default/files/resources/SAS-GLASS-Gender-HB.pdf**

IANSA Briefing Paper 20 September 2021 Strengthening the Connection Between Small Arms and Light Weapons Controls and the Women, Peace and Security Agenda https://iansa.org/wp-content/uploads/2021/10/Strengthening-the-Connection-Between-Small-Arms-and-Light-Weapons-Controls-and-the-Women-Peace-and-Security-Agenda-ENGLISH.pdf

Small arms and light weapons, gender-based violence and domestic violence: analysis of regulatory framework and practice August 27, 2021 UNDP Serbia https://www.undp.org/serbia/publications/small-arms-and-light-weapons-gender-based-violence-and-domestic-violence-analysis-regulatory-framework-and-practice

Measuring the impacts of small arms on war zone and post-conflict VANESSA FARR societies https://www.iknowpolitics.org/sites/default/files/conflicts_pg26-31.pdf

Gender Perspectives In Arms Control And Disarmament Views From Africa Workshop Report United Nations Institute for Disarmament Research UNIDIR https://unidir.org/sites/default/files/2020-05/Gender%20Perspectives%20in%20Arms%20Control%20and%20Disarmament%20-%20Views%20from%20Africa.pdf

Gender and Armed Violence Reduction in West Africa Mines Advisory Group - November 28, 2022 https://reliefweb.int/report/world/gender-and-armed-violence-reduction-west-africa

Gender and SALW Gender Aspects of SALW and How to Address Them in Practice SEESAC 2018 https://www.seesac.org/f/docs/Gender-and-Security/Gender-Aspects-of-SALW----ENG-28-09-2018.pdf

UNDP 10-Point Action Agenda for Advancing Gender Equality in Crisis Settings https://www.undp.org/sites/g/files/zskgke326/files/2022-11/UNDP-10-Point-Action-Agenda-for-Advancing-Gender-Equality-in-Crisis-

Settings.pdf

The Sustainable Development Goals Report 2022 https://unstats.un.org/sdgs/report/2022/The-Sustainable-Development-Goals-Report-2022.pdf

Effective Weapons and Ammunition Management in a Changing Disarmament, Demobilization and Reintegration Context: A Handbook for United Nations DDR Practitioners Department of Peace Operations Office for Disarmament Affairs New York, 2021 Second Edition https://peacekeeping.un.org/sites/default/files/ddr-handbook-2ed-3_2021.pdf

Gender and Armed Violence Reduction in West Africa 2022 Lessons learned from weapons and ammunition initiatives MAG https://www.maginternational.org/media/filer_public/d6/09/d609452e-bc52-4e08-bfbd-fcbcadf48bb7/gender_and_diversity_in_salw_in_wa_1122.pdf

Also by Uwem Essia

Gender and Arms Control in Africa

"Gender and Arms Control in Africa" offers a comprehensive examination of the intricate interplay between gender dynamics, arms control, and peace in the African context. With insights derived from eight chapters, this book scrutinizes the impact of arms proliferation, the role of women's NGOs in post-conflict recovery, and the significance of gender-sensitive disarmament programs. It delves into the influence of media, emerging technologies, and mentorship initiatives in shaping the arms control landscape. As the first of its kind, this book unravels the complexities surrounding the Women, Peace, and Security (WPS) agenda, offering a roadmap for fostering security, equality, and sustainable peace across Africa.

Gender Dynamics in Armed Violence, Small Arms Control and Security

"Gender Dynamics in Armed Violence, Small Arms Control and Security" is a compelling exploration into the critical issues of Small Arms and Light Weapons (SALW) proliferation and its intersection with gender-based violence. With a nuanced and multi-dimensional approach, this book navigates through the far-reaching implications of SALW in post-conflict societies while highlighting the Arms Trade Treaty's role in addressing gender-based violence. It unravels the complexities of gender in arms export decision-making and offers practical insights into gender-responsive small-arms programming. Drawing on the United Nations initiatives, it underscores the gender dimensions of small arms control and suggests transformative interventions. This thought-provoking work is an essential resource for scholars, policymakers, and advocates striving for a safer and more equitable world.

Discover the critical role of Women's Security Awareness (WSA) in conflict recovery with this groundbreaking book. "Women Security Awareness in Conflict Recovery Programs" explains the unique vulnerabilities women face in conflict zones, from exacerbated gender inequalities to limited access to essential resources. This comprehensive guide outlines the transformative power of WSA programs in empowering women and strengthening community resilience. Learn how these initiatives provide tailored interventions for immediate safety while influencing long-term, gender-responsive policy planning. With a focus on agency, autonomy, and multi-stakeholder collaboration, the book offers a blueprint for integrating women's security concerns into broader conflict recovery strategies. Essential reading for policymakers, NGOs, and community leaders, this book is your roadmap to creating more equitable, sustainable solutions in conflict-affected areas. Unlock the potential of empowered women as drivers of change—read this book to take the first step.